I am so proud of my brother's new book *Unexpected Places*! Reading about Anthony's unexpected places allowed me to reflect and recall the unexpected situations in my own life that have played a part in who I am today. This book is an exhilarating ride that will help any reader learn how to expect the unexpected and truly appreciate this ride we call life.

—Jonathan Evans, speaker, author, and chaplain of the Dallas Cowboys

As a fellow pastor's kid, so much of my friend Anthony Evans's story resonated with me. It's a unique peek at what it looks like to navigate one's own faith and find one's own voice, trying to handle the pressures and expectations that come with all of that. Specifically, as you read about how doors opened in real and unexpected places, you'll be strengthened by Anthony's faith and encouraged by the reality of God unfolding in his life. I'm grateful for his genuineness and for the risk he's taken here in this book to tell his story on behalf of so many.

—Judah Smith, Lead Pastor, Churchome

Honest, introspective, and charmingly personal, *Unexpected Places* is a behind-the-scenes journey through ministry, music, and personal memories as my brother Anthony tells his story. More than a memoir, this book holds Anthony's hard-earned perspective on how the need for significance, success, or a second chance can shape an individual and delivers valuable life lessons to benefit any reader. Even though I've had a front-row seat to Anthony's life for most of my own, this book still surprised and delighted me; I'm sure it will do the same for those who, like me, find themselves enjoying the pages of Anthony's eye-opening and extraordinary adventure.

—Chrystal Evans Hurst, bestselling author of *She's Still There*

Unexpected Places is just what you want and need from a book: it's honest, it's moving, and it's hopeful. The way Anthony writes is so fun and entertaining, but it's also incredibly encouraging. I have been impacted by the story of what God has done in Anthony's life, and I know you will be too. Don't miss out on the opportunity to read this book!

—Chad Veach, Lead Pastor at Zoe Church in Los Angeles

We absolutely love Anthony with all our hearts and have been honored to share real life with him for years. His humor, authenticity, and honesty is so refreshing; you will definitely be encouraged by his heart and stories.

—Jeremy and Adrienne Camp, recording artists,
authors, and founders of *Speaking Louder*

Anthony is a once-in-a-lifetime kind of talent. You probably know him from his ability to sing a song and communicate it beautifully with precision, honesty, and emotion. But as with every song, you only get about a five-minute window into Anthony's soul. With this book, however, you get a lifetime. It's filled with treasures of truth, memorable moments of joy and pain, and an in-depth look at a man doing his best to please God with his life. I got to know Anthony during the "Nashville" phase of his life, and I couldn't be more proud to relive some of these memories with him (and learn a few things I didn't know)! Try putting this book down. I dare you.

—Michael Boggs, singer and songwriter

Anthony Evans is one of the most sincere and heartfelt individuals I know. We've all heard it in his worship, but I've been privileged to see it come to the fore firsthand in his interpersonal relationships. We are all familiar with Anthony's unmistakable voice in song, but in *Unexpected Places* he introduces us to his voice beyond song—a voice that is completely worth tuning in to hear as well.

—Justin Ervin, award-winning filmmaker

PRAISE FOR *UNEXPECTED PLACES*

As a leader in the church, one of the first obstacles you have to overcome is the lie that you're supposed to be perfect. That you can't let others see your faults or your wounds. Anthony Evans has given a true gift to current and future members of God's kingdom by showing us his story and his heart in such a moving way. Read this book, cherish it, and then pass it on to someone else who needs this kind of honesty and wisdom in their lives!

—Christine Caine, bestselling author,
Founder of *Propel Women* and *A21*

What happens when you combine a big heart with an amazing voice and a bright smile with an incredible mind? You get Anthony Evans—my dear friend. You are going to love his book. Wonderful story. Wonderful man.

—Max Lucado, bestselling author, speaker

I had the pleasure of having Anthony on my team during Season 2 of *The Voice*, and I knew from the moment I heard his voice during the blind auditions that he had something very special; I later learned he has a heart of gold to match. That combination will no doubt take him far in his career, and he will always have me as a fan in his corner.

—Christina Aguilera, singer, songwriter, and actress

I am excited for my son's new book *Unexpected Places*! Unexpected, that's just how the Lord works. He has a plan for us, and we are called to stay open. It is so important to remain close to His heart so we can be aware of His will for our lives and in turn walk confidently into these Unexpected Places.

—Dr. Lois Evans, author and speaker

God rarely leads us from where we are to where we need to go in a straight line. It usually takes a zigzag course for us to develop into the people we need to be. In my son Anthony's new book *Unexpected Places*, he lets us travel through the zigzags of his life so we can see how God has taken him to the place He wants him and is using him in the way He wishes.

—Dr. Tony Evans, bestselling author, radio personality,
and Senior Pastor of Oak Cliff Bible Fellowship

For 20 years now, Tammy and I have been privileged to see the behind-the-scenes journey of Anthony becoming the phenomenal man he is today. As his "play" big brother and sister, we are well aware that the natural and spiritual components of who we are and what we're created to be can make the navigational process problematic at times. Anthony has been given a multiplicity of gifts, so the question of "Lord, what shall I do?" often gets answered only when He leads us into that Unexpected Place.

—Kirk and Tammy Franklin, recording artist, author, and
creative director of Fo Yo Soul Entertainment

Anthony's story deserves to be told. Even more, it deserves to be told like this: in his voice, from his perspective, owning his truth. I've always been proud of my baby brother for bravely following his dreams, pursuing his passions, putting in years of hard work to reach his goals, and, most importantly, honoring his faith in God. That's why this book is important. First, because you'll really get to know the man behind the beautiful voice. Second, because it will inspire you to find your own in a world that is constantly telling you to quiet it. I assure you that the book you hold in your hands will be a journey worth taking. So enjoy every page.

—Priscilla Shirer, bestselling author, Bible teacher,
occasional film actress, and proud big sister

I've known Anthony Evans for the better part of two decades. Anthony is hyper-intelligent, incredibly kind, and of course immensely talented. He's also very honest. Never one for spiritual platitudes or Christian clichés, his is a quest for an authentic journey with Jesus. *Unexpected Places* is a candid and compelling story of an imperfect man following a perfect Savior.

—David Hughes, Lead Pastor of Church by the Glades

UNEXPECTED PLACES

UNEXPECTED PLACES

THOUGHTS ON GOD, FAITH, AND FINDING YOUR VOICE

ANTHONY EVANS

with JAMIE BLAINE

W PUBLISHING GROUP

AN IMPRINT OF THOMAS NELSON

Published in Nashville, Tennessee, by W Publishing, an imprint of Thomas Nelson.

Thomas Nelson titles may be purchased in bulk for educational, business, fund-raising, or sales promotional use. For information, please e-mail SpecialMarkets@ThomasNelson.com.

Library of Congress Control Number: 2018901258

ISBN 978–0–7852–1931-6
ISBN 978-0-7852-1940-8 (eBook)

Printed in the United States of America

18 19 20 21 22   LSC   10 9 8 7 6 5 4 3 2 1

To my parents, for living by example and letting me come to the conclusion on my own that there is nothing in life I want to be more than . . . just like you.

CONTENTS

CONTENTS

PART 3: HOLLYWOOD

CONFESSIONS OF AN ADD PK

Behold, I am doing a new thing; now it springs
forth, do you not perceive it? I will make a way
in the wilderness and rivers in the desert.

—Isaiah 43:19 esv

I'm driving down Sunset Boulevard, talking on the phone with the Christian book publisher, trying to find the studio so I can arrange vocals for a hot rap artist's new number one project. Man, who am I kidding? I'm trying to find myself. Just like all these beautiful LA people in all these beautiful cars around me.

Red light. I look around and everybody's on the phone. Everybody's texting. Everybody looks anxious. I need to respond to a text. Two texts, actually. Another just came in. I need to hit that one back first. While I'm talking to the nice person from the book company. While I'm thinking about getting coffee and what time I have to meet my trainer at the gym. And what am I gonna eat for dinner tonight?

The Christian publishing people want me to write a book? Me? Really?

"Hello . . . ?"

The call must have dropped. Reception is terrible in the hills. I need to pull over and find a better signal.

Be still and know that I am God.

I'm trying to be still, Jesus! I'm trying.

I have ADD. Attention deficit disorder. I am the guy who goes through life, every few minutes like—squirrel!

See, I did it again. A squirrel just ran through Plummer Park, and he took my whole train of thought with him. Plummer Park, that's where the old retired guys play dominoes. There's a farmers market in the side parking lot every Monday. I exercise in the park sometimes. I messed up my knee there once and had to have surgery.

That's a picture of what my attention span looks like. Me, write an entire book? Yeah, right.

How did I get this way? Was it my parents' fault? My teachers' fault? TV's fault? God's fault? The Devil's fault? My fault, somehow? At the end of the day, does it matter?

Moses was a stutterer. God met him where he was and used him anyway. Samson had anger issues. He still made the Faith Hall of Fame in Hebrews 11. King David, he had all kinds of emotional turmoil and still managed to be a man after God's own heart. He even wrote about his problems in all their honest, messy truth—and God put it in the Bible!

Just one of the ways the upside-down kingdom works. Our

weakness is His strength. He is glorified in our infirmities. He uses our failures to draw all men unto Him.

The light turns green. Big-money motorcycles zip between the Beamers and Mercedes-Benzes. I text back quickly: *On my way.* The squirrel runs across a power line while my phone tells me to take a right on Gower Street. Bold white letters on the side of a hill proclaim HOLLYWOOD. Everything you've heard about is here—secret sins and paparazzi, celebrities and wannabes, drugs, sex, and billion-dollar homes.

And right smack in the middle of it all? A shy preacher's kid from Texas. This is the last place in the world I thought I would end up. But I can say without a doubt, in this season of my life, this is where God wants me to be.

I get a better signal and the book publishing lady calls me back again. "Yes ma'am, I'm in," I tell her, my voice raspy from overuse. "I'm willing to give it a try."

What do I need to say? Want to say? Feel called to say? The wheels in my brain begin to turn. . . .

I want to be honest from the get-go. I'm the guy who will count the pages of a chapter before I even start to read. If it's too many, I'm easily distracted and overwhelmed.

So, in some ways, this book is written for my attention-deficit brothers and sisters. The sections are a little shorter. Sometimes I get right to the point and other times I get sidetracked and ramble a bit. There are lessons learned from dark days and troubled times, stories from confusion and pain.

But there's funny stuff too. You gotta laugh. That's what life is.

Laughter and pain, doing your best to find the balance between all the things you can and cannot change.

Hopefully, prayerfully, you'll come along for the ride. Because even in my darkest moments, I came to realize I can bring God the crazy, messed-up pieces of my life and trust Him to turn it into something that people will be drawn to, something worthwhile, something that would convince you that He wants to do the same for you.

This is a book about the unexpected and unplanned, a loose collection of stories, thoughts, and memories. It's a journey out of darkness and back to life. And isn't that the story of most of our lives?

Fonzworth Bentley, a network executive producer, calls again. I answer and he starts to speak at a record pace before I can even say hello—all about singers and song parts and the studio's budget. A light on my dash flashes. The sensor says my back tire is slowly going flat, but for now it's safe to keep driving on. I can sure relate to that.

PART 1

DALLAS

CHAPTER 1

NEVER BE HIM

Blessed are all who fear the LORD, who walk in obedience to
him. You will eat the fruit of your labor; blessings and prosperity
will be yours. Your wife will be like a fruitful vine within your
house; your children will be like olive shoots around your table.
Yes, this will be the blessing for the man who fears the LORD.
—PSALM 128:1–4

There were sixty-three thousand men gathered in Texas Stadium, fathers and sons shouting and chanting and stomping their feet. They were not there to cheer on Troy Aikman and the Cowboys against the 49ers. They had come to hear about the importance of integrity, honor, and keeping one's word. A football stadium jam-packed with men all yelling for Jesus.

August in Dallas is blistering hot. I was twelve years old at the time, sitting in the backstage area, waiting. Dad often wanted me to tag along for ministry trips, and his recent stint with Promise

Keepers had already taken us to Los Angeles, Kansas City, and Detroit. Nearly a million men attended the Stand in the Gap conference at the mall in Washington, DC. It's crazy watching one million people listen as your dad speaks. I was glad to be back in Dallas, closer to home.

A rumble echoed through the giant arena as the lights went down. My ears and cheeks burned as the rumble turned into a roar and they announced his name.

Tony Evans. That's me. His name is my name too.

There were blue-shirted ushers everywhere with Promise Keepers tags around their necks. As Dad began to speak, they looked from him to me. Smiling. Nodding.

And all the expectations that come with carrying that name.

I sat listening as my father preached, challenging men to stand strong and stay committed, to guard their hearts and families with their lives. Reminding them we can't just call ourselves Christians and not be men of character and truth. They weren't just empty words. If anybody knew that, I did. Dad lived what he preached.

Every man in that building was on his feet, many with hands lifted, crying and saying, "Amen." The air was charged with hope as he brought his message to a close.

"If you want a better world made of better countries . . ."

The sound of Dad's voice boomed through the corridors and off the concrete walls.

". . . inhabited by better states, made up of better cities that are illuminated by better churches made up of better families—you have to start by becoming a better *you*."

As the crowd shouted their approval, I shrank back, looking for a place to hide. Though thousands were stirred and encouraged by his message, I could only think one thing:

I can never, ever be him.

CHAPTER 2

GROWING UP EVANS

Children, obey your parents in the Lord [that is, accept
their guidance and discipline as His representatives],
for this is right [for obedience teaches wisdom and self-
discipline]. "Honor [esteem, value as precious] your father
and mother" [and be respectful to them]—which is the
first commandment with a promise—"so that it may go well
with you and that you may enjoy long life on the earth."
—EPHESIANS 6:1–3

Preachers' kids are often a bit off, some even a couple degrees
from crazy as they try to find their own way. My dad is Dr.
Tony Evans, founding pastor of Oak Cliff Bible Fellowship in
Dallas, Texas. For the past forty-two years he's preached all over
the world, having been heard on the radio, seen on TV, and even
authored more than one hundred books.

My beautiful mother, Lois, has stood right beside him and sup-
ported him every step, running the business of ministering behind

the scenes. Eventually she started her own ministry, reaching out to pastors' wives. As parents go, they're pretty amazing.

There are four of us kids. Chrystal, my oldest sister, is the brainiac. Totally analytical and a great help to me as she develops her own writing and ministry. Then there's Priscilla. She's Ms. Personality. Growing up, Priscilla talked a whole lot and sometimes it would get her in trouble, but it seems to be working well for her now. She's all across the country, speaking and writing bestselling books. You may have seen her starring in the film *War Room*. Number one at the box office!

My baby brother, Jonathan, he's super logical, an excellent businessman, and a devoted husband and father of four. Jonathan signed to play for the Dallas Cowboys and then later became their chaplain.

And me? I'm the sensitive one. I might look like a grizzly bear, but some days I've got the emotions of a teddy bear. Artists are just weird like that. It's part of the deal. Which works great when it comes to music and leading worship—but honestly? Sometimes those same emotions can overwhelm me.

* * *

"What was it like growing up as Tony Evans's son?"

That's the first question church folks usually ask me. Some people are looking for dirt, I think—to see some ugly picture behind the scenes or to find out the famous preacher is a hypocrite at home. It sounds a bit silly to say, but most of the time, living in the Evans house felt like a Christian version of one of

My family: me, Priscilla, Mom, Dad, Chrystal, and Jonathan

those eighties TV shows where trials were always an opportunity for life lessons, the family pulled together, and things turned out okay in the end.

As a kid, you take everything for granted, but now I realize how much work it took for my parents to be as solid as they were while running such a big and busy ministry. Oak Cliff Bible Fellowship was already blowing up by the time I was born, so I never knew anything different. Truth is, if there was one problem for me growing up as the son of a famous pastor, it was this: I wasn't all that crazy about church.

I'm not talking about *the* church. I loved God and Jesus and God's people. I just wasn't a big fan of church activities twenty-four hours a day, seven days a week.

Every child has their own particular struggles and sensitivities.

I was the introverted Evans kid—the one who needed a lot more one-on-one time but who was too shy to speak up and let anybody know. And when your dad is the preacher of a giant church? You are around people *all the time*. Every day there are a bunch of people at your house. Or you're over at theirs. There is always a wedding or a funeral or a revival or a church dinner going on.

Preachers' kids are expected to be pretty much perfect—to be seen but rarely heard, to always take a back seat to the needs of the church. My parents didn't put that on me, but I definitely felt the pressure all around. Over time, I developed a smoldering resentment. *Leave my dad alone. Leave mom alone. Leave us alone and let us be normal people.* He has to be "Pastor Tony Evans" all day. Can't he just be ours on nights and weekends?

But that's not how it works in ministry. You share your parents. Nights and weekends are when all the crazy stuff happens. Emergency room visits. Married couples fight. Some new convert has a crisis of faith. The church drama queen has an "urgent need" to share somebody's business so you can pray. Somebody's old uncle gets drunk and out of hand.

The needs were always imperative, and who did they call? What's the church version of *Ghostbusters*? My father. Didn't matter if it was nine o'clock at night or four in the morning.

To add to the tension, we lived across the street from the church, so people would just randomly show up at our door. I would open it quick and tell them nobody was home. Someone would call asking for Pastor Tony—and I would straight hang up on them. *Don't bother my dad.* Later, after puberty hit, I would lower my voice and pretend to be him. "I'll have to call you back," I'd say in a rush, ending the conversation before they had a chance to speak. (I don't think he ever knew this. Sorry, Dad!)

Somebody was always wanting something from my parents, but I felt like I needed something more. There were many other pastors to choose from. I only had one dad. And I didn't feel like I should have to apologize for needing time with him.

Our church kept growing. Hundreds became thousands. The load got even heavier and the needs louder as my parents tried to stay on top of things. Dad's desire was for Oak Cliff Fellowship to be known as the "little big church." Regardless of the size, people weren't numbers, they were individuals, and he felt like it was important to know each and every one.

I mean, my parents started Oak Cliff in their tiny apartment from nothing. Dad wanted it to remain personal. On an everyday basis, you don't realize the toll it takes.

I understand that now. But as a child? You can't process events that deep. A six-year-old is not going to ask his mom to go to counseling so they can discuss how to voice his needs. My personality is a people pleaser and peace keeper. I always wanted to be an asset and never a burden. I wanted my presence to be associated with ease and a smile no matter the cost.

It wasn't my parents' fault. Because I was so quiet, they thought I was the simplest kid in the world to deal with, when really I was just keeping it all inside and looking for other ways to bring attention my way.

Here's one example: The Christian academy I attended was very strict. Students were expected to be focused and obedient at all times. There was a girl in my class named Cece Roberts, and I went through a phase where I would chase her around nearly every day, teasing her and pulling her hair. Acting all crazy even though I knew good and well there would be a spanking coming my way after school.

"Just wait till your father gets home, Anthony!" Mom would say. I think I was subconsciously figuring out that negative attention was better than none. You wonder why so many preachers' kids misbehave? That might be your answer right there.

Once I grew up, I learned that resentment is pretty common among children whose parents are in full-time ministry. I realized I was not the only one.

CHAPTER 3

THAT'S THE WAY

Whatever your hand finds to do, do it with all your might.
—Ecclesiastes 9:10

I was charging across the pasture on a pony named Grey Sky at
Pine Cove Camp, a Christian retreat in Tyler, Texas, out on Lake
Palestine. Dad was a speaker there every summer, which allowed us
some really great out-of-the-box experiences.

I'd been going to the camp since I was three, and by the time
I turned eight, Pine Cove was my most favorite place on earth.
They had skate parks and climbing walls and zip lines over the
water, and the counselors there always had the enthusiasm and
time to teach a young boy about the love of God through the
beauty of nature. If I was hungry for attention, Pine Cove provided a feast.

It was a perfect summer day, and I was looking at the tall pines
between Grey Sky's ears, the lake shimmering in the distance.
Then Grey Sky seemed to be going one way and me another. Next

thing I knew I was slipping sideways. Then all of a sudden—*bam!* Down I went.

I tumbled through the dirt and laid flat, staring at the sky. *What?* I thought. *Why am I on the ground?* Involuntary tears started to flow because of the shock. I think I also added a bit of dramatic crying and breathing to the moment because I knew a bunch of attention was coming!

A commotion followed, counselors running my way. Next thing I knew, a tall, bowlegged cowboy grabbed me and hauled me to my feet.

"There, now," the cowboy said, dusting me off and checking to make sure I was okay. "You don't look too much worse for wear now, do you?" He smiled and stooped down to eye level. He had a big straw hat and stubbly beard. His face was weathered, but his eyes seemed kind.

"No, sir," I managed. "I'm okay." Falling was more of a shock than an injury, so I met his steady gaze and gave back my best eight-year-old, rough-and-rugged cowboy nod.

"Atta boy," he said, holding out his callused hand to shake. "I'm Mr. Tim. But everybody calls me Swanee 'round here." He led Grey Sky back to the barn, loaded me up onto his horse, and handed me the reins. "You know what we gotta do now?" he said, nodding back. "Right?"

Little did I know that falling off a horse would result in meeting one of my most important mentors in life. God was turning my fall into a moment of grace.

"Right!" I replied.

After that, Swanee was always happy to see me. And once I was old enough, he was ready to put me to work around the stables. I wouldn't be at camp five minutes before he would start handing me buckets of feed to haul or a rake to gather up hay. His thing was to teach the kids biblical principles through practical application, which helped me a lot more than any lecture ever did. The best part, though, was when we got to work directly with the horses.

"See that one over there?" he told me during one visit a few years down the road. "That's Pilgrim." Tethered to the fence was a short, stocky, brown-and-white Paint Horse that clearly had a Napoleon complex. He was thrashing around wildly and snorting, pulling against his restraints. Swanee wasn't being cruel. A horse, even a little one, has to be gentled before you can let them work with kids.

"I named him Pilgrim because he's got a lot of progress to make before we can use him," Swanee said, chewing on a long piece of hay. "But he'll be okay. Soon Pilgrim will figure out that resistance to his master only causes pain. Similar to the kind of pain we feel when we don't listen to God. Resistance to Him only makes our lives more difficult, and it brings us that much more confusion and pain."

I stood at a distance, watching Pilgrim twist and pull, a thousand pounds of sheer energy and rage.

"We train a horse to trust his master and let him lead the way," Swanee continued. "Horses can be stubborn. They want to run when they want, eat when they want. But by trusting the master's plan, all their needs will be supplied. They'll live a good life, and through their obedience, others will be blessed. But they have to learn to trust us first. Sometimes that's a long, hard process."

I watched Pilgrim pull back, buck and snort and fight that fence post, thinking about all the ways I resisted God's plans—all the ways I didn't fully trust and obey Him yet. I thought I knew about horses by that time, but Swanee's lesson was something new. Resisting the process made Pilgrim that much more miserable. And it was that much longer before he could be used in service. But Swanee and his team of wranglers were patient. They wouldn't give up. They would keep on working with Pilgrim until his training was complete.

Even though Swanee was head wrangler, he wasn't above doing the lowest job. He'd always say, "Whatever you put your hand to, do it with all your might and do it right." I think he saw I could be a bit distracted, so he was always looking for ways to teach me excellence by example, to push and challenge me in my relationship with God.

If something wasn't right, we'd do it over and over again. If I

Swanee (Tim Alderson) and me

saddled a horse and made a mistake, he'd call me over. "Anthony, what's wrong with this picture?" he'd ask. Sometimes I'd stare at those straps and the cinch twenty minutes trying to figure it out. Eventually I got better and better until one day Swanee hired me on to help part-time.

Swanee would be at the stables at four every morning, and I was right there with him, getting the horses ready before our breakfast trail ride at seven a.m. One time the horses had been out all night and one Palomino, Patience, was particularly coated in dirt. It was more than obvious that she had decided to roll in mud—it looked like she had played in it.

Swanee handed me a curry comb and put me on one side, and he took the other. "Now, Anthony," he said, "the objective in this exercise is to get this horse cleaned up and ready to work. I am going to do it with you, and when we finish, I expect your hands to be every bit as dirty as mine."

I started combing my side of Patience, but it was hard going. The dirt was embedded so deep in her coat that I didn't seem to be making any progress at all. Swanee let me struggle at it for a while. Finally, he looked over Patience's flank and showed me a better way. "The combs go in a circular motion," he said, demonstrating as he spoke. "We gotta stir the dirt up to the surface first in order to get her clean. And Anthony, when the dirt is embedded this deep, it's gonna take a lot of effort to get it to the surface. It's the exact same way we have to admit to and talk about our own shortcomings in order to get our hearts clean. We've got to let Him bring all that dirt to the surface first and deal with it for what it is."

Watching Swanee closely, I copied his motions until clouds of dust started forming around Patience's body and settling on our skin. Together, we worked the entire horse. By the time we finished, we were both covered in dirt, but Patience was clean and shiny in the morning sun.

We stood shoulder to shoulder for a minute, admiring our work. I looked down at Swanee's filthy hands. Then I held up my own. They were just as dirty as his. Swanee smiled, slapped my back, and we coughed in the dust. "Yes, sir," he said with a nod. "That's the way it's done."

CHAPTER 4

PATIENCE FOR THE PRACTICE

Jesus replied, "No one who puts a hand to the plow and
looks back is fit for service in the kingdom of God."
—LUKE 9:62

For the first few years of school I made As and Bs and didn't get my first C until all the way in sixth grade. I thought maybe it was a freak accident, but then more Cs started coming my way.

Oh my goodness, I thought. *I'm average.*

About that same time, Dad's speaking ministry was taking off and he was gone a lot, flying around the country for events. Mom sometimes went with him, and while they were away, I stayed with my aunt Elizabeth, better known as "Auntie." Eventually, it was just more convenient and beneficial for me to go to school closer to where she lived. The schools there had an excellent reputation, and my parents believed it might help improve my studies.

The school board required students to live in the district for a certain number of nights in order to be eligible, and my dad didn't want to lie. So, I started to spend a lot more time at my aunt's house to make sure we were following the school board's rules. In Dad's mind, it was a functional and practical decision because I was staying with family. He was giving his son a great education, and it worked out because I was staying over there a lot anyway. I wasn't crazy about the arrangement—I would have preferred to stay at home—but it was more important to me to keep the peace and not cause any trouble.

Seventh grade was an interesting transition. Up to that point, I'd been attending a small, conservative Christian academy. Next thing I knew I was in a new district and thrust into a whole new world—public school with a thousand kids where I didn't know one soul.

It was the early nineties in Dallas, and style was crucial to your social status. Even at the Christian school, we made sure those polo collars were starched down and our khakis were rolled just right. The girls wore asymmetrical bangs and side ponytails, and the boys wore their hair strategically cut, edged, or gelled and sprayed back like it was our glory. Because it was a Christian school, of course, you could only go so far with fashion statements. Even at that age, they taught us there was a fine line between being current and carnal.

The thought of going to a public school for the first time was scary. As a preacher's kid, the last thing I wanted was to be seen as someone who didn't know style. On the days leading up to the first week of school, I carefully planned out my outfit. Khakis were out of the question. I needed to look *cool*.

The kids were going to laugh me out of the building if I

walked in looking like I did at the Christian school. One night, it came to me. I was lying in bed staring at the ceiling and suddenly I just knew. Who was the coolest, most stylin' human being on all of God's green earth? Probably in God's whole universe? Well, in 1991, the answer to that was easy.

The first day of school, I put on the outfit I'd planned over the previous week and checked myself out in the mirror, touching up my hair with my Andis T-edge clippers. Perfect.

My aunt dropped me off at the front door and I glided through the schoolyard with my head high. Kids everywhere were staring. *Yeah!* Then I noticed some of them were giggling. *What's so funny?* Nope, scratch that. A *lot* of them were pointing and laughing out loud. That's when my heart began to sink.

All the other students were wearing acid-washed jean shorts, white tennis shoes, and tucked-in T-shirts. I was decked out in MC Hammer pants, dress shoes with no socks, and a rayon shirt topped off with a perfect high-top fade featuring not one, not two, but *three* "I'm in public school now" lines shaved into the side of my head. I had never seen these movies because I wasn't allowed, but I figured public school was like the *Boyz in the Hood* and *School Daze* movie trailers I had seen on my "you're allowed to watch TV" nights.

My aunt's car was long gone. Once you get to school, it's too late. I was stuck dressed like MC Hammer in a sea of students that looked like they had just stepped off the set of *Saved by the Bell*. Which I was not. Because when the bell rang, there was nothing I could do but head to class.

Welcome to your first day of public school, church kid. It's Hammer Time.

After making it through eighth grade (barely), I started classes at Duncanville High. I signed up for football right away, but I had something of a lazy streak. I would join the team, then quit, then rejoin and quit again. Then change my mind and ask to sign up once more. Anytime my father saw a tangible need, he would show up and be supportive. But after a while the back-and-forth got old. "Come on now, Anthony," he said. "What's going on here?"

Dad drove down, re-signed the permit forms, and I gave football one more try. I loved playing the big Friday night game under the stadium lights, but those two-a-day practices every day? Nuh-uh. As an offensive lineman, I was bored out of my mind. So, I would give nothing in practice and still expect to be put in the game. Lesson One that I would later implement in the entertainment business came early: *Don't expect to play the game if you don't have patience for the practice.*

Duncanville High had a state champion music program—as a matter of fact, Duncanville was the state champion at just about everything—but I really didn't do anything but sing a little in the church choir back then. And in the car, of course. My friends thought it was hilarious that I could sing along with the radio and hit those really high notes. That's what I liked, the high-pitched pop singers like Whitney and Mariah Carey, Brian McKnight, BeBe and CeCe Winans, and Boys II Men. I even had an En Vogue poster on my bedroom wall, hidden behind the folds of the curtain. Dad wasn't super legalistic and I didn't think he would care, but just in case. . . .

Once you became an upper classman, Duncanville had a vocational career and technical program where students could get hands-on training for a specific job. Graphic arts, welding, health science, fashion design, cosmetology, culinary arts. Due to my experience with Pine Cove Camp, I chose the agricultural program.

At the end of the day, for my seventh and eighth periods, I would drive out to the school barns and my favorite teacher, Mr. Baker, would help me raise Milo, my goat, and Rawhide, my steer. Instead of giving some mind-numbing lecture while writing stuff on a blackboard, Mr. Baker would get his hands dirty right there next to me, just like Swanee back at Pine Cove.

I got to do everything related to farm business, from buying to showing livestock to selling on the back end. I was amazed that school could be something I loved and looked forward to every day.

I could still be introverted sometimes, but Duncanville helped me slowly come out of my shell. It opened me up to a lot of diversity too. At school lunch, I would go from table to table, able to have a conversation with just about any group—the FFA crowd, the athletes, the band kids. I didn't fit into any one group. I fit a little into all the groups. It's cool to look back and see how my career and ministry were being formed long before I began to notice.

Even though I didn't participate in any of the music activities at Duncanville, I can see how God was developing my voice, but also my desire to connect outside of what was expected of me. How He took an uncomfortable situation and made something positive out of it, even though my attitude was sometimes bad. Although I loved her deeply, I wasn't crazy about staying with my aunt Elizabeth or the fact that my parents were sometimes traveling, and I still didn't always understand. I just wanted to be in *my* room playing video games. But looking back, I can see where it all worked together for good.

I just hated that right as I was starting to love school, it was all about to end.

CHAPTER 5

ALREADY GOOD

Therefore, brothers, be all the more diligent
to confirm your calling and election, for if you
practice these qualities you will never fall.

—2 Peter 1:10 esv

I graduated from Duncanville High School, drove away from campus, and cried my eyes out—two things heavy on my mind. First, most of my close friends like Casey, Brian, Kyle, Brandee, Charlene, and Josh were juniors, and I was wishing I had failed twelfth grade so I could stay back and chill with them for another round in the Duncanville Duffers (a sort of fraternity of guys that assisted and escorted the cheerleaders and occasionally performed skits for the pep rallies. I don't tell many people that because they all say, "You were a cheerleader?!").

Second, the thought of "what's next" was seriously freaking me out.

My plan was to attend Texas A&M, major in animal science,

and eventually become a large animal veterinarian. I know most people would never think that about me, but growing up, it was the only thing that could hold my attention. Being with Swanee in the barn as a child ignited a love for the biology, breeds, and nutrition of large farm animals. I thought I had my future all mapped out, but when I sent my transcript, Texas A&M was like: *Uh, thanks, but no thanks, Anthony Evans Jr. We don't care if you're Jesus Jr. You do not have a future at Texas A&M.*

I tell people that the Aggies' admission office went on strike in 1996. (I think they actually did.) But in reality, I couldn't focus long enough through high school to make the grades. I guess I should have tried applying at a few other schools. Again, the focus thing.

So instead of going to my dream school for my dream career, I ended up at a Christian college in Lynchburg, Virginia, that I had absolutely no desire to attend. The only thing I knew about Liberty University was that I had to wear slacks and a tie to class, be in my room by eleven every night, and make my bed when I woke up. These were not good things to know. Suddenly I was wishing I had devoted a little more time to my studies. It looked like I'd be one sad dude leaving high school *and* arriving on my first day of college too.

When I say "ended up at," I mean my amazing father had helped find a way for me to go to Liberty University. All I had to do was sing.

"Wait. I gotta do *what?*"

"Sing your way through school, son," Dad shot back. "And then you won't have student loans hanging over your head for the next twenty years."

Let me backtrack for a minute. Singing started later in life for me. I mean, I sang around the house some, but I definitely wasn't one of those five-year-old kids performing "Jesus Loves Me" on the platform as his stage parents/the pastors watched while mouthing every word. Because I wasn't passionate about singing, my parents didn't give it much thought. Until I turned seventeen and Dad started connecting the dots, submitting a VHS tape from one of my church performances and making under-the-radar phone calls to Liberty's chancellor, Dr. Jerry Falwell.

(My father *loves* connecting the dots for people. Especially his kids. It's one of his "spiritual gifts." To this day, he will cross his arms, laugh, and tell me, "You know I made your career, right?")

I made my trek to Lynchburg and immediately entered a rigorous rehearsal schedule. Because I was late, I had to spend two or three hours a day learning the fourteen-song set the other singers already knew. I had to get fitted for four suits. We wore matching suits! Seventeen years old and wearing matching suits for a Christian college singing group. Man, that was every bit as cool as it sounds.

What I didn't realize was the Sounds of Liberty was the school's flagship group that sang everywhere, all the time. They had even sung at the White House. I had to perform constantly. On campus, there was no escaping being recognized because Liberty was so small. They would announce me from the stage as "Tony Evans's son!" It pushed that old raw nerve in me. My name is his name. Performance equals acceptance. The load of expectations I can never fulfill. That was my whole life—practice, performance, putting on the show. I was quickly overwhelmed.

I wanted to leave Liberty *so* bad. It sure didn't feel like liberty to me. I felt trapped. I had no desire to disappoint my parents or let the group down, but I didn't want to be featured on stage as Tony Evans's kid. I wanted to be somewhere studying animal science and not wearing suits, just trying to figure out who Anthony Evans Jr. was supposed to be.

I sank further and further into depression, trying to make everyone happy but me. I missed Texas. I would call my house in Dallas with nothing to say but just wanting to hear someone's voice from back home. We'd be on the Sounds of Liberty tour bus, fifteen college kids riding across the country, playing Uno, laughing, sharing life—and I would be sitting off by myself, staring out the window for hours at a time, thinking, *What am I doing here? Why am I singing southern gospel songs at God Save America rallies?*

The group, especially my closest friends, Matt and Mark, started to catch on that something wasn't right. My mood swings got so bad that one of the other members finally asked, "Do you think you might have a chemical imbalance?"

I sat in my dorm room at Liberty and realized that every last thing I believed was because my church and family told me to believe it. It's like I was really just God's grandkid, not his child. But God doesn't have grandkids. There are only sons and daughters. Second-generation faith is never enough.

I think the depression set in because I wasn't ready for that much responsibility. I had to be a spiritual leader and smile like everything was fine, when I felt like someone who had never picked up a weight but was expected to go for the world-record bench press because his dad was an Olympic lifter. I had to act like a natural when it felt completely unnatural. I had to step up, lead, and share, all the while wishing my father had named me Scooby or Snoop or Larry or anything other than Junior.

I had to pretend and keep my pain a secret. And secrets make us sick.

After a long, weird year, I went home for the summer, glad to let go of the weight of all those expectations. I spent all of June and July back at Pine Cove in the barn with Swanee, trying to regain my sanity. Two months wasn't long enough, and August rolled around way too fast. I gathered up some courage and looked Dad straight in the eye. "I am not going back to Liberty."

"Oh, yes you are," he replied.

I didn't skip a beat. "No, sir. I'm not."

Never in my life had I back-talked my father like that. He got this really intense look on his face, like steely-eyed and carved from stone. Like Moses probably looked when he came down from Mt. Sinai. You preachers' kids know what I'm talking about.

Welp, this is it, I thought. *Guess I'm about to die.*

Dad studied me for a while, not saying anything. I must have said those words with conviction, because he read between the lines and realized there really was something wrong. Discernment, I think they call it. Thank God.

Much to my surprise, he let me make my own decision even though it sounded like a foolish mistake. I dropped my scholarship at Liberty and went back to the woods to work as an intern at Pine Cove Camps. No more stages. No more matching suits. All I had to do was help my old friend Swanee take care of the horses, make sure our campers were happy and safe, and be on call for any needs.

I was sort of like a glorified ranch hand, but I was content. There was a lot less pressure out there in the wilderness.

One morning I was out at the stables grooming my horses, Homeboy and Atlas. Right on the other side of the fence was one of the cows who had just given birth. I watched as her brand-new baby calf tried to walk. His legs were weak and wobbly, and it took a lot of stumbling and falling down before he got the hang of it. Swanee taught me many lessons at those stables, but now he was hanging back, watching. I wasn't a kid anymore. He was waiting for me to get the revelation for myself.

Finally, it struck me. Me and that wobbly calf had something in common. The only way to build up strength and stability was to learn to get your legs up under you and walk on your own.

I had never done that. Between my home family and church family, I'd been sheltered. My father and mother had always provided me with everything I needed. True faith was a foreign concept to me. Somehow, I needed to learn how to walk on my own. But knowing something and doing it are two entirely different things.

A few days later, Dad called to check in with me. It was good to hear his voice, but I didn't know what to say, so I mostly just listened. He could tell I was still struggling, I'm sure.

"Son, have you ever read Psalm 128?" he asked.

"No, sir."

He read me the part about how a man who fears the Lord will be blessed, his wife a fruitful vine and his kids like olive trees around his table. At first I thought, *The Bible says I'm an olive tree? That's kind of strange. . . .*

Then I looked it up. Turns out olive trees are crazy strong.

My parents and me

They can survive most anything. Even if lightning strikes the tree and burns it to the ground, it can still come back to life. Olive trees can produce a harvest for centuries to come. They're very versatile: the wood, the leaf, the fruit.

I realized that because of my parents' faithfulness, the burden to be okay wasn't all on me. I didn't have to have everything figured out or pretend to be doing better than I really was. God would help, and there was grace for the messed-up parts. It didn't matter whether I was singing to a thousand people or shoveling out stables. It wasn't about what I was doing. It was who I belonged to. I was already good.

I hung up the phone and walked back out to the barn. I saddled up Atlas and rode down to where the trail passed by Lake

Palestine. Taking a leap of faith means we face the things that scare us. Sometimes it means we back up and give it another try.

After a semester in the wilderness, I took those matching suits out of my closet and drove back to Lynchburg, Virginia. Going back to Liberty felt like my own decision this time. When you're a teenager, that always helps. I began to get my legs up under me and learn to walk for myself. Soon enough, my feelings started to follow my feet. I was singing, rehearsing, doing everything the group asked—but instead of seeming like a burden, it was more of a joy.

Isn't every college freshman a little bit immature? Some of the most important stuff you learn in college doesn't happen in a classroom. Like persistence and sacrifice and how to make it on your own. How to get along with others.

The discipline and accountability of being in the Sounds of Liberty turned out to be really good for me. Sometimes God takes us the long way through the desert before we're ready. He's in no hurry. One thing God's got plenty of is time.

By senior year, I had developed a full-blown passion for singing. I felt like it was a gift from God and He wanted me to use it for good.

I finished out my time at Liberty University and graduated with a degree in youth ministries. I'd like to tell you it's because I felt called in that direction, but to be honest, even though I love kids, I was just looking for a major that didn't have much math.

I was still trying to get my wobbly legs up under me. I still had a lot to learn.

CHAPTER 6

TRUTH IS . . .

Consider it pure joy, my brothers and sisters, whenever
you face trials of many kinds, because you know that
the testing of your faith produces perseverance.
—James 1:2–3

After Liberty, I was asked to join a well-known contemporary
Christian group called Truth. Truth was a vocal ensemble
and full band founded in 1971 that consisted of fifteen to twenty-
two members at any given time and was soon to be inducted into
the Gospel Music Hall of Fame. I was offered a verbal agreement
for a two-year deal.

Truth stood for **T**rust, **R**eceive, **U**nchangeable, **T**rue **H**appiness
[in Jesus], and the Sounds of Liberty was a picnic compared to the
workload there. We toured nonstop, over three hundred concerts
a year, sometimes doing multiple shows in the same day. When we
weren't on the road, we were making records. There was not much
pay. We were often expected to work for free.

One of my first experiences with Truth was walking into a room at an extended stay hotel. I was trying to figure out where I was going to sleep during our first week of rehearsals, which I had heard would be intense.

Having been given a room number at the hotel, I wandered the halls until I found my door. It was open. Inside, there were three guys I had barely just met, sitting around talking and laughing. A quick look around the room and I could see it was pretty standard. There were two doubles, a small table with two chairs, and a TV stand. I let my duffle bag drop to the ground at my feet. They looked up when they noticed I was taking up most of the doorway and blocking their light.

"Hey," I said a little nervously, wondering why there were so many people in my tiny room. At the same time, I was looking forward to getting to know these people I was about to spend the next two years with. They seemed like a fun group so far. "Where are you guys staying?"

They answered together. "Here!"

I dropped my other bag. "Oh!" I said as normally as I could. "That's awesome!" Inside, though, I was wondering how that would work exactly. I eyed the double bed closest to the door. I shuffled in and found an empty spot for my stuff. We had a long road and a lot of practice ahead.

Since the hotel was extended stay, housekeeping only came once a week, so if we wanted to make sure we had a dry towel—or even the same towel that we had started the week with and not someone else's—we had to figure out how to claim it. Hang it on a hook in the closet. Over the back of the same chair. Whatever you had to do to remember where you left it.

It was the same thing with the side of the bed you were on. If you wanted your share, it had to be claimed—never mind actually being able to sleep through the snoring. (Okay, I'll take my share of the blame here.) And I won't even go into the details of what sharing a bathroom was like after a week in the same room with four dudes fresh out of college.

Man, it was tough. But I know now that if I could handle that, I can handle anything. What doesn't kill us makes us stronger, right? Somehow, we made it work. But I won't lie, there was a lot of prayer involved about my own attitude.

Once we started performing, we didn't have to rely on the extended stay hotel anymore. Every night we'd stay at a host home, which was supposed to mean clean sheets and fresh towels. Every now and then, I'd even get my own room. Those times were pure gold! But of course, staying in a different person's home every night had its own set of challenges.

God's people are so generous and good, but getting into a car to go home with a complete stranger is always a roll of the dice. We went in twos for safety. I guessed that was in case somebody at the host home was a mass murderer, the other one of us could run and tell, "So-and-so's dead!" I'm kidding, of course, but there were some weird nights that made you sleep with one eye open.

Most nights it would be a friendly family with an average-sized home and a clean room to go to, but there were times when we'd pull up to some small, dark trailer and not know what to expect.

Once inside, we would be given the only bed available while the owners slept on the couch. They literally gave us everything they had for the night, which was amazingly kind. But as a guest, it's hard to feel good about that.

One morning, after meeting back up at the bus, a couple of the girls in the group were pretty upset and reported that they had been taken to a tiny singlewide the previous night, arriving late after the show. They were already thinking that there couldn't possibly be any space for them when the mother called into a pitch-black room and ordered her children out of their bed so the young women from Truth could climb in. The kids sleepily crawled out of their well-worn nest and went to sleep on the floor in a pile of blankets.

Other times you would round the corner into a neighborhood and have no idea you were about to make lifelong friends with your host family. And not because they had the greatest house but because they had the greatest hearts. Anytime we toured Florida, I'd think, "Thank God, I get to stay with the Lovelands!" And any-time we went to Georgia, it was like, "I can sleep at the Sniders'!" They were like an oasis in the desert for me.

Nearly twenty years later we're still connected. I knew their kids then, and now I know their kids' kids. Those relationships are the rewards I left with from all the times I lay awake staring at the ceiling to a trio of snores with a bathroom in the corner of the room that was more like a science experiment than a place to get clean. Those are the God-given treasures that I claimed.

Life on the road took some adjustment, but in the end, I am grateful for the lessons God showed me during that time. He taught me to be thankful and to never take anything for granted.

Even those times when people gave up their own beds, leaving us to feel uncomfortable and wishing desperately that we could be the ones to sleep on the floor—I had to learn that generosity works both ways.

One of our commandments in the Bible is to be friendly to strangers, and our sweet host families did just that. There were many times when I found myself thinking about what it must have been like for Jesus and the disciples as they traveled. Were they offered other people's beds? Would they have said "no thanks" if a family was doing their best to give them everything they had, even if it meant putting their own kids out for a night or two? Or did they let people serve, receiving their humble gift with grace, because they knew this allowed the giver to increase in their own generosity and grace?

For me, being offered someone's bed while they slept on an air mattress or sleeping bag became less about my own discomfort and more about allowing others to shine. Because those moments weren't about me but about them. Because what those people were doing was beautiful. I am humbled by their selfless acts to this very day.

CHAPTER 7

AND THE TRUTH SHALL SET YOU FREE

Do your best to present yourself to God as one
approved, a worker who does not need to be ashamed
and who correctly handles the word of truth.

—2 TIMOTHY 2:15

I met some close friends and developed a good work ethic in
Truth, but I also learned to associate ministry with acting like
everything is fine while running yourself into the ground. Clean,
Christian living was achieved by staying too exhausted and busy to
get into any mischief.

There were no set hours. You never complained, never said no.
That's how to have a servant's heart. Do exactly as you are told.
Never question anything. Be thankfully submissive at all times, or
else you are out of God's will.

If you talked about struggle, it was something vague and

fully conquered through prayer. Specific sins were not discussed. Nobody spoke of sexual struggles or depression or substance abuse. There was no safe place to admit you sometimes struggled even to believe.

Over time the grind began to wear me down. Touring in a band doesn't build character, it reveals it. I was still sensitive and insecure about so many things. The work seemed endless. There were days when I was sure if I kept pushing I would damage my throat. But the notion was that if you buckled under the load, you were ungrateful, lazy, and they would just find someone younger and more willing to take your place.

After all, we'd all just been invited to be in an act that was literally spinning off Christian pop stars. The group before us had Natalie Grant in it. 4Him came from Truth, as well as two of the singers who ended up being in Avalon. And now we were on that same track to "success." If we just put in the time and effort, we could make our mark on the Christian music industry too.

I wasn't trying to be rebellious, but sometimes I needed help to understand. If something seemed unfair, I couldn't just sit by in silence. Our director quickly grew weary of my attitude and constant inquiries about what was happening. He would just look at me and shake his head. "You ask too many questions," he would say.

But I wasn't the only one who felt that way. There was trouble brewing behind the scenes. A lot of nights we would put on our game face for the crowd only to collapse later, completely burnt out but too intimidated to object. The illusion has often been created in Christian music that service always comes first, even if it's tearing you apart inside.

One day, after a string of back-to-back shows, I was feeling sick and my body was begging me to slow down. I had gotten to that dangerous place again—anxious, exhausted, emotional, and overwhelmed. Sick or not, I still had to unload an eighteen-wheeler, set up the stage, get dressed, perform like everything was great, tear the stage down, pack the gear back in the truck, and hit the road. Then do it all again the next day. And the next. All for a paycheck of fifty dollars a week? Come on.

I was sitting in the dressing room of one of the many churches we were scheduled to perform at that year, quiet and keeping to myself. I guess my demeanor came off sour, like I didn't care. I wanted to be respectful and appreciative, but sometimes, when you're hurt and dog-tired, things don't come out right.

The director marched up, stared me in the face, and told me I was worthless, lazy, and wouldn't ever do or accomplish anything better than where I was in that moment. I sat there, stunned, not responding. I guess I was still naïve enough to think everyone in Christendom was soft-hearted and super nice.

"This is as far as you will ever go," he continued. "You will never be anything more in the music business than this."

I held my tongue, nodded, and finished getting dressed. Then I did the show, loaded up the gear, and climbed into my bunk on the tour bus. I had a lot of miles to ride and think it over. If this was the definition of "ministry," I wasn't sure I wanted any part of it. If being exhausted, emotionally crushed, and manipulated was what this was about, then—I'm good. No thanks.

If God made me go, I would go. But if I had any choice in the matter, I'd rather have headed back to Texas and lived out on some ranch riding horses and raising cows, where nobody knew me and nobody cared whether I was on a stage or not. Why is success in ministry always measured by how busy you are? Didn't Jesus rest? Didn't He say He would give us rest and peace?

There's that old saying about sticks and stones, but in all honesty words do hurt, and I often find myself thinking about them for a very long time. Words mess with my head. But I get to choose how to react. I could use the situation as a reason to quit or an inspiration to press on.

Somewhere on that bumpy road between Atlanta and Little Rock, I made a decision. I didn't have to let anyone else but God decide what ministry meant for me. I could submit to authority and I could work—but still find a way to move forward by my own convictions.

Calling me worthless may have been based on that moment because of my mood or attitude, but it wasn't who I was. One person's opinion did not define me. My foundation of faith and family was stronger than that.

Sometimes we need an enemy more than a friend. Friends can placate us and tell us what we want to hear, but it's often criticism that motivates us to change. Kind words soothe us. Opposition stirs us to action. David's allies didn't make him king. Goliath did. Joseph didn't become second in command in Egypt because of his strong family—in fact, his family opposed him.

Our director was given authority over the group, but he was not given my destiny. I would prove myself worthy and that I *did* have a future in the music business. And who knows? Maybe the director saw that I needed my buttons pushed more than a pat on the back. Or maybe he was simply having a bad day too.

I slept through the night as the miles passed. Everything seemed clearer the next morning as we pulled in behind the gym at San Dimas High. I unloaded the gear, put my show clothes on, did my job and sang unto the Lord and not unto men. And then I broke down the stage, loaded the truck, got on the bus, and did the next show. And the next. I decided I would be obedient, to do my best to rise above.

There were times when I questioned my decision. I loved singing for the Lord, but some days I became impatient to spin off and do my own thing. A few times I even got a call from Kirk Franklin—a trailblazer in the music industry and a friend—asking about my status with Truth.

"Are you done yet?" he would ask.

"No, not yet," I would say, secretly wondering what would happen if I quit to go on the road with him. It was next level, and I craved it. But I had made a promise that I would be faithful to my commitment, and I was going to see it through. Besides, I wasn't one hundred percent sure Kirk wasn't just being nice. He was on top of the gospel music charts, working with the best of the best. Why would he want me?

One time he called and asked if our singing group would accompany him on his upcoming album. He wanted the look of many different races and different people and thought Truth was the perfect group to back him up. I went and talked to our director, totally excited and sure I had good news.

"No way," he replied.

A bit surprised, I asked him why.

"Too much time for practice involved," he said. "Financially, we wouldn't be able to support ourselves. Three weeks of rehearsal would kill this group."

I didn't understand why it would be so hard to make the finances work, but it wasn't my decision. Feeling defeated, I called Kirk back and let him know the verdict. If I hadn't blown it before, I was sure this was the final nail in my coffin. There was absolutely no way I would ever work with Kirk Franklin after turning this down.

And so I stayed and pressed on for another year and a half with Truth. Crazy as it sounds, things eventually got better. Even that same director who called me worthless made me road manager for the band. The guy (me) who pushed back and tried to take the group in a different direction became the one trusted to run the daily affairs. Funny how it works that way.

We finished up the tour, and at the end of my two-year commitment, the group called it quits. After thirty years on the road, Truth had finally come to the end. Only it was not really the end. Instead of cutting us all loose, we were all offered an additional six months to do a farewell tour. It was up to us to decide at that point if we were in or out.

I had stuck it out that long, so I figured I could go another six months. We had done six hundred shows over the course of two years. It would be hard to go another mile, but I could do it.

Then one of the young women announced that she was not staying, and that's when things fell apart. We were so closely knit together as a group that when one left, it all started to unravel.

Soon it became a mass exodus. I held on to the very end, but when everyone else started to bail, I had to ask myself why I was so set on gritting my teeth through another run. Besides, the biggest Christian artist in the world had stayed on me and said to call him as soon as I was done.

I thought back to the determination I felt after the run-in with my director. I was not going to be a failure in music. I was going to succeed. I was going to put my faith in God and not in my fears or hang-ups.

I said good-bye to Truth, realizing that as I did so, it really was the end of an era. In some ways we had grown as close as siblings in that time, and I wasn't sure how I was going to go forward. Music was changing. Times were changing. I was changing too.

I left a message for Kirk that I was out of the group, not knowing what he might say. For all I knew, he didn't have an opening for me anymore. I got on a bus and headed for home. As I crossed the state line, my cell buzzed. I answered it.

"Hey, my brother," a familiar voice said. "Did I hear you might be looking for a job?"

Less than a week later I was in rehearsal, and soon after that, on a plane to London.

CHAPTER 8

REBIRTH

A friend loves at all times, and a brother is born for adversity.
—Proverbs 17:17 esv

London, England, Royal Albert Hall. It's my first show with Kirk Franklin to promote his *Rebirth* album. He's number one on the gospel charts, has the number-one hip-hop/R&B LP, and has certified gold and platinum sales.

Kirk's hometown is Fort Worth, Texas, and he started going to our church when he was eighteen. So, I had known him for quite some time. Musicians often talk about working together down the road. Usually it's just that—talk. But Kirk made good on his word.

Royal Albert Hall is a sell-out, fans on their feet and hands in the air. On the opening number's downbeat, Kirk greets the UK audience with, "Lemme hear you say 'lovely day'!"

I take a deep breath and start to sing my part. From my station near the rear of the stage, I'm amazed by the size of the crowd and the room. With all the tall gold arches, red carpet, and purple lights, the place looks more like a king's palace than a concert hall. But the way we're singing praises, I guess it is the King's palace, at least for one night.

It seems like a dream. After all those years, here I am, singing the songs I know and love with Kirk. Not in the crowd watching. On stage! It's humbling and empowering at once, like when you turn sixteen and you'd be happy with any old run-down beater, but your dad hands you the keys to a brand-new car instead.

I would have taken a run-down singing career. I could have accepted not even singing anymore. But here I am standing in London's finest arena, singing with the best performer in the business. It is as if God has yelled "Surprise!" and given me a car straight off the showroom floor.

Kirk closes the show with his Grammy-nominated song "Lean on Me." I know my part and perform it, standing out of the spotlight with the other nine background singers.

The music swells as we arrive at the big ending. Kirk stops, looking around until he catches my eye. Then he waves for me to come to him. My heart sinks. I know what this means.

In my previous experience with Truth, everything was strategically rehearsed and planned. We knew exactly when and where each portion of the show would happen. But gospel music is different, like spontaneity is a byproduct of soul. Kirk's concerts went by feeling, led by the Spirit, often going off script.

In the past, from the audience, I had watched Kirk randomly hand over his microphone to one of his background singers to sing the last lines of the song. But surely he wouldn't do this to me in my first show. *Would he?*

I rush to him. "Sing the hook, Anthony," he tells me, pushing his mic into my hand. "Land the plane. You take us home."

I stare at the microphone, feeling its weight, paralyzed with sweaty palms and poker-face fear. A room full of five thousand people are screaming, waiting to see what I will do.

I have to make a decision quickly. Am I confident enough in my abilities to be spontaneous? To even *attempt* to take on Bono's part and sing the final lines of this legendary and much-beloved song? *How do you land a plane that you've never flown before?*

I consider my options—I even consider faking being too overwhelmed by the Spirit to sing, crying, shaking my head, and handing back the mic before retreating to my spot toward the rear of the stage. But then I remember that part in the Bible that says be ready, in season or out. Stay alert because you never know when your time will arrive. All those years of singing in groups and on stages, of endless rehearsal and going through the motions of stuff that I felt didn't matter—in all of that, God was preparing me for a moment such as this.

I step into the spotlight and raise the mic. The crowd sings along, swaying side to side. "Here's my shoulder. You can lean on me."

Kirk nods and whispers to me. "Take your time, Anthony." Which in Kirk's world means, *sing it again.*

I repeat the line, riffing on the melody, the crowd singing louder each time. Finally, the band slows down and brings the song to an emotional close. The people erupt as Kirk literally jumps on my back, pumping his fist in the air.

It feels like I passed some sort of test. I did it. I led us all home.

CHAPTER 9

MY LIFE IS IN YOUR HANDS

I've put my life in your hands. You won't
drop me, you'll never let me down.

—PSALM 31:5 MSG

My next gig with Kirk after London was at the Grammy awards in Los Angeles. Kirk didn't explain why we were there, just to show up and meet him at a certain time.

"Anthony, come with me," he said when I got there. He led me around the back of the Staples Center, through the maze of walkways lined with dressing rooms labeled with the names of everyone at the top of music. We rounded a corner, and there was a group of guys standing around looking cool in their shades and leather jackets.

Wait, that dude in the red sunglasses kinda looks like. . . . And that one over there with the black cap—hold on. Seriously? I'm standing backstage with freaking U2?

The band was nominated for eight Grammys that night and

would be opening the televised portion of the show. An assistant led us to a room where we practiced vocals for a song called "Walk On," from their latest record. It talked about how we're all packing a suitcase for a place we haven't yet been, how before you can see it, you have to believe. Bono sang "hallelujah" a lot with his hands lifted high. It sounded like gospel music to me.

U2 were sweet and down to earth, very complimentary of the vocal stylings we were adding to their song. The Edge gave me his guitar pick. I wanted to be professional and not come off like too much of a fan. From unloading an eighteen-wheeler into a high school gym to backing U2 for the Grammys! Life is so crazy sometimes.

For the next four years, Kirk and I were rarely apart. Stellar Awards, Dove Awards, BET, *The Tonight Show*—we performed everywhere, all over the world. He really is the most gifted performer and songwriter I've ever worked with. And despite all his talent, he is truly an authentic man.

At one point I traveled with Kirk for a show in South America. On the flight down, I wasn't exactly sure what to expect. Had the people even heard of Kirk Franklin down there? I assumed he was doing some small church a favor, maybe putting on a charity concert or something like that.

On the plane, I did my best to get comfortable in seats that were built for people half my size. I slept when I could, and in my waking moments I thought about a recent offer I'd received to record my very first solo project.

After many hours in the air, the plane finally touched down on the runway and slowed to a stop. I figured we'd lug our suitcases

Kirk and Tammy Franklin; my sister Priscilla and me

to our ride at a chill pace and get to the hotel where I could stretch out and stare at the ceiling for a few.

Daylight flooded the cabin as a flight attendant pushed open the door. The sticky, humid air hit me halfway down the aisle. I was standing just a little behind Kirk in the aisle, fighting to get my overhead luggage out of the bin. There was nothing I wanted more than to get off that flying soda can. Slowly, passengers started to exit down one of those tall staircases they roll to the airplane door.

Exhausted, we grabbed our bags and made it through customs. I walked out through the automatic exit doors, trying to get to the van as quickly as possible. A loud racket broke loose. Thinking something was wrong, I stopped and looked over to see a huge group cheering.

Kirk started waving to the crowd. They were chanting his name, pressing in closer just to catch a glimpse of him. I followed behind him, grinning in disbelief. From their enthusiasm, you'd have thought Justin Timberlake had just arrived. *The church we're singing at must be bigger than I thought.*

Caught up in the excitement, I started waving too. *Unbelievable!* I thought to myself. *All of this for us!*

We made our way through the crowd. The people pushed in closer, reaching out. I reached back, shaking hands. One woman had clutched onto Kirk's coat sleeve, tears in her eyes.

My suitcase caught and I stopped to fix the handle so the wheels would follow right. A few people from our crew politely passed, separating me from Kirk. I stood back up, eagerly expecting the crowd around me. But all I saw were backs turned my way. They'd all left me behind.

A stray dog passed, stopping just long enough to shoot me a look like, *Who are you? And more importantly, do you have any food?*

Reality check. I had to laugh. These people were here for Kirk, not me. I smiled and hung back. "Every moment you're trying to teach me something, aren't you Lord?" I whispered as the dog ran away.

After a stop at the hotel, we were taken to the back of a rickety old building. We entered through a creaky door and walked down a half-lit hallway to our dressing room. It was small, with cinderblock walls and worn-out couches.

I thought about the crowd that had met us earlier—sorry, the crowd that had met *Kirk*—back at the airport, and I figured maybe there'd be at least a few hundred folks who loved his music enough to show up.

We waited for our cue and walked back down another dark hall to the stage. I could hardly believe it. The arena was ginormous. I made my way to my place on stage and looked out to a sea of golden brown people, eyes shining with the love of the Lord.

I was nearly too awestruck to sing as Kirk started the show. The audience knew the words to every song even though we were singing in English. Later in the concert we started into "My Life Is in Your Hands," and you could feel it in the room, something special was going on.

Suddenly the people began to sing the lyrics back to us in Portuguese. It's an incredible experience to sing about God in a country that doesn't speak your language. To see them respond even though they cannot understand, you realize that the love of God goes beyond language.

We tried to finish the song, but the people would not let us end it. Kirk called the translator over. "I want everybody in this room to know that you can never go so far," he began, "that you can't come back home."

From the floor to the balcony to the rafters, every hand was lifted, reaching, swaying side to side. "So don't just sing it to sound good," Kirk told the people. "Sing it from your heart. Because when we sing from our hearts, we get God's attention. He comes down to meet us right where we are."

Thousands of voices sang back in their native language. Kirk started to direct us, and we did our part in English with the audience echoing it back in Portuguese. Scarcity creates gratefulness.

Even though a lot of the people of Brazil didn't have much, I could tell their lives were full.

Seven minutes in, we were singing softly as the band brought the music low. Kirk called me down front. I stood beside him (looking a little like Shaquille O'Neal duetting with Prince) as we sang the chorus again. The entire arena sang with us. Kirk handed me the mic and stepped away.

I don't speak Portuguese, but someone in the audience was shouting out words to me. *Estou em Tuas mãos.*

I sang that phrase over and over, praying I got it right, that I wasn't singing "I love barbequed goat," or worse, accidently saying something profane. There was a hush across the room, tears flowing, thousands worshiping in spirit and truth. That huge concert hall got small. Small and big at the same time, if that makes sense. Small and intimate as people in one accord, but big as the God of the universe. I told Him that if I never had anything else in my career, this one pure moment was enough.

Kirk taught me that's what mattered most. Not the crowd or the stage or the status of your accommodations or bank account. It's that moment of connection between you and the people and God in heaven above. When for just a little while, we are all one and the same.

"My life is in your hands." That's what I was singing. For those precious few seconds, I believed it with all my heart. Whatever else was going on in my life, I knew that was the truth.

CHAPTER 10

THE SHOW GOES ON

Better is open rebuke than hidden love. Wounds from a
friend can be trusted, but an enemy multiplies kisses.
—PROVERBS 27:5–6

Touring with Kirk was a master class in performance and ministry. He always stressed that the person you were for those twenty-three hours *off* stage was just as important as who you were for that one hour on stage. Anyone can get up there and pretend for a while. It's who you are out of the spotlight that matters, how you treat the people at the drive-thru window when you're getting coffee or the housekeeping staff at the hotel. Gospel music can't be measured solely in record sales or how much the industry or the fans accept you. Whether you're accepting a Dove Award or working in the plumbing section at Home Depot, there is always something more. God is constantly teaching and refining us through our circumstances.

One night we were doing a show in Chicago. I'd been with

Kirk a few years by that time. A friend of mine lived in town and had a performance scheduled for later that day. He's an incredibly talented artist, and I really wanted to go hear him sing.

"Yo, Anthony," my friend said, "you sure you can make it back in time for your show?"

"Yeah," I answered, "I think so."

What I didn't know was that Soldier Field, the stadium where the Chicago Bears play, sat in between where my friend's concert was located and the venue where I was performing with Kirk. The Bears game went into overtime. Traffic was backed up for miles. Kirk could have started the concert without me but waited instead. Which meant everybody waited. The band, the singers, the audience. We were playing in a theater that was under union rules, meaning the times to begin and end the show were extremely rigid. Which meant my act of selfishness cost him a lot.

I walked in, and everybody on the tour was in a big prayer circle. Except me. Kirk just gave me a disappointed look like, *Really, Anthony?*

That look broke my heart. I went to support a friend, which is great, but I knew I was cutting it close. By being inconsiderate, I had trampled Kirk's grace.

It wasn't a matter of forgiveness. It was a matter of losing my place. Kirk had taken me around the world and shared his stage, even letting me sing my solo songs on the biggest gospel tour on the planet.

I took his blessing for granted. I was wrong, and my actions likely cost Kirk thousands of dollars. I didn't do it on purpose. I don't know that I felt some sense of entitlement, but that's what my actions sure showed. And that's what mattered.

After the show, he called me into his dressing room and sat me down. "I cannot work with you in this capacity anymore because you have taken advantage of my kindness."

He talked like it hurt to say the words. They hurt both ways, I guess.

"I'm so sorry," I said.

"I love you, brother," Kirk told me. He set his hand on my shoulder. "But maybe it's time for you to go off and do your own thing."

Kirk let me know the show could go on without me. I had not been needed—I had been wanted. The only righteous response to that is gratitude.

A lesson from the kingdom again. I cannot earn a place on God's team. He doesn't need me to keep the universe turning. I am saved and forgiven because I am wanted by Him.

Once I had to make it on my own, I realized how much Kirk had been fighting and providing for me. His lesson still sticks with me today. It's one of the reasons I am blessed with so much work. I understand that with or without me, the show can still go on. So, I am grateful for every opportunity. If I'm working, it's because somebody wants me around.

Kirk Franklin remains my mentor and biggest influence in the business. More importantly, he remains my friend.

PART 2

NASHVILLE

CHAPTER 11

BIG HIT LIFE

It's obvious, isn't it? The place where your treasure is, is
the place you will most want to be, and end up being.

—Matthew 6:21 msg

I started making trips to Nashville while I was still with Kirk to check out possibilities for my own career. Nashville seemed like a magical destination, like that pirate ship the Goonies found in One-Eyed Willy's cave. It was packed with treasure for the taking, and all you had to do was get on board and claim it for yourself.

Initially I stayed with friends like songwriter Jason Ingram and his wife, Culley, sleeping on floors and couches. Jason would go on to win SESAC and Dove Awards, but at the time he was just getting his own career off the ground. Still, he would put himself out there to tell people about my singing.

Just as I'd hoped, Nashville proved to be treasure-filled. Because of Jason's help, I got signed to a deal right away, started writing songs, and made my first record, *Even More*.

Even More produced a top-ten single, "Here's My Life," but the label had hoped for more. The problem, they said, was that my music had too much soul for contemporary Christian radio yet wasn't soulful enough for gospel. Contemporary was the richer target, and there were many suggestions on how to retool my image to give it more CCM market appeal.

"Here, strap on this guitar," one Nashville executive told me.

"But I don't play guitar," I replied.

"Oh, we won't plug it in. Just hold it while you're up on stage. Everybody's doing the guitar thing these days."

I wanted to be a team player. If you're difficult to work with, they'll pass you by for someone more willing to bend. These were Nashville pros, and they'd been in the business a lot longer than me. At that moment, it didn't feel like I was selling out—it's just that I sincerely didn't know what to do.

I wrote with different artists and worked on changing my sound. I lost weight and tried different clothes. I was still touring with Kirk Franklin on the weekends while he searched for a replacement, and then I was flying in and out of Nashville during the week to work on my solo career. I wanted to show the industry that I was an artist worth investing in and believing in.

For my second record, *Letting Go*, they kept my picture off the cover, hoping maybe music buyers wouldn't stereotype me by looking at my face and automatically assuming I was in the "black gospel" genre. We used a lot more guitars, some distorted and others jangly, as was popular in hit Christian music at the time. There were no chart singles, and the record did not perform well. I was trying to fit the mold and it didn't come across as genuine. For a project called *Letting Go*, it was pretty uptight.

"Probably for the best, son," my father suggested. "If that record would've been a hit, you'd be stuck singing those songs you didn't love for the rest of your life."

Dad had a good point, but it didn't make me feel much better. I was fighting that old fear of being unaccepted again, trying to prove my worth. But I figured one failed project wasn't reason enough to quit. I wasn't going to give up that easily on my dream.

"If you really want to make it in the music business, you gotta live in Music City." I heard that piece of advice over and over again. So after my time with Kirk ended, I bit the bullet, packed my stuff, and moved to Nashville.

They were right. Things got better. And they also got much worse.

●   ●   ●

Nashville is known for country music, but truth is, nearly everything Christian comes from there. Books, music, movies, major ministries. Look on the back of most any Christian product, and you'll find the words *Nashville, Tennessee.*

Melissa, an old friend from Truth, had been recruited into one of Christian music's biggest acts and lived in town with her new husband, Ben. They graciously offered me their spare bedroom until I could find a place of my own, so I moved in with the newlyweds and started trying to make connections with the singers and groups I admired in the industry. I thought all Christian artists were exactly what their music portrayed. If I heard a hit song, I assumed their life was a big hit too. Now that I lived in Nashville, I was ready for the big-hit life to come my way. I was willing to do whatever it took to find my place.

I pursued relationships based on status and public persona. In hopes of being valued, I compromised my convictions and often devalued myself. I tried to be whoever people wanted me to be in an effort to win their approval.

Music City could be dangerously alluring for someone as naïve and insecure as me. Soon I became caught up in a very dysfunctional and codependent group and found myself in the strange position of having to keep secrets about some of my favorite Christian artists.

On one hand, I felt hugely blessed to have these people as mentors and friends. On the other hand, it was just really weird. Addictions, pretension, conflicting lives. The term *performer* was key. Life behind the scenes was not always the big, beautiful hit the image portrayed.

It's easy to get caught up in the whirlwind. For a highly emotional person like myself, the highs are too high and the lows too low. Long story short, I trusted the wrong people, fell in with the wrong crowd, and got taken advantage of emotionally, spiritually, and financially. I don't want to play the victim or sound judgmental. I don't need to name names. I'm only trying to explain. I was a grown man in his mid-twenties, yet I had the perception of a sixth grader. Sometimes when you want something really bad, you ignore the truth.

Ironically enough, my music career had started to improve. I was getting booked to lead worship and sing solo shows around the country. My name was getting out there. Still, it seemed like there should be something more to life. So, I decided to take the biggest leap of faith yet.

Leading worship is both a passion and a calling.

CHAPTER 12

BROKEN

The LORD is close to the brokenhearted and
saves those who are crushed in spirit.

—PSALM 34:18

There's this thing Bishop T. D. Jakes says from his pulpit down in Texas: *Before I can trust you, show me your scars.* I mention my broken engagement in concerts and church services a lot as part of my testimony, but really, I avoid the details because it still hurts. But a friend of mine says a good book is like two people talking one-on-one, just from me to you. And in a good book you take a deep breath and do your best to tell the simple, straightforward truth as you see it. So here goes.

Everybody told me that when I went off to college—especially a Christian college like Liberty University—that's where I would find my wife. "The One." That Perfect Mate God Made Just for Me.

In the Christian world, that's how it goes—that's just the way we talk. College for church kids can be stressful. It's where you're supposed to find your spouse, your purpose, your ministry. To mature firm in the faith and get your whole life plan figured out. All in those four crazy years.

Sure enough, when I came back for my second semester, it wasn't long before I found myself mesmerized by a co-ed with super-curly hair and an athlete's build. We didn't have any classes together, but our paths crossed now and then.

I was scared to talk to her. There was something regal and confident about the way she carried herself that intimidated me. One afternoon I was hanging out with my Sounds of Liberty friends at our regular spot by the coffee shop in DeMoss Hall, and she walked right up to me. "Hey, I'm Andi." She stuck out her hand. "I wanted to come over and meet you."

"Umm, Anthony," I replied, unable to hide my big, nervous smile. "How are you?"

We talked for a minute before I floated my way to Apologetics 201 on a cloud, still smiling. She was confident, all right. Strong and assertive. Turned out she was an athlete for the Liberty Flames.

We spent the next few months slowly getting to know each other. I could tell she wasn't very impressed with me at first, but then one night we were at a friend's house, just talking. And we kept talking. About God, life, the Bible—everything. Silly stuff, deep stuff, hopes and dreams. The next thing I knew, the sun was rising. We had talked all night.

It sounds crazy now, but the whole time I was thinking, *These are exactly the kind of conversations I want to have with my wife!*

From that moment on, we grew tighter. Well, as tight as we

could. At Liberty, hugs over three seconds were basically not allowed. Hand-holding was the only appropriate form of personal contact. It was considered improper to be alone after dark with members of the opposite sex.

But that wasn't necessarily a bad thing, because it forces you to focus on bonding emotionally and spiritually with a person instead of letting the physical stuff confuse your heart and mind. Physical attraction is important, but it makes a poor foundation for a relationship.

So, we just kept talking and spending time together in other ways. We would go out to eat, catch movies, hang out with friends. There was that perfect fall night we went to Scaremare, Liberty's version of a Halloween haunted house. I was expecting some cut-rate cheesy Christian rendition, but it was really good and scary. Huge, too, all through the woods and into an old mansion. It was nice to see that Christians could put on such a quality production.

One of my professors had told us that Scaremare was where a lot of students take the next step in their personal relationships and that they'd even had marriage proposals happen right there on the front steps of the haunted mansion. As we held tightly to each other's arms and edged past the giant creepy rabbits and wicked clowns, I thought maybe it was time for Andi and me to take the next step in our relationship too.

But there was always that voice in the back of my head saying: *You will never be good enough for her. You're going to fail her and her family and your family and everybody. You will mess things up, Anthony. You always do.*

It was a lot of pressure, being pulled both ways. Looking back,

I should have been able to recognize the lie of the enemy, but I couldn't figure out how to deflect it in its time. I questioned my ability to step up and be the person she needed me to be. I didn't have the confidence Andi did. I felt sure that if she got to know me too well, she would only be let down.

So instead of pressing in and being vulnerable, I would get weird and withdraw.

We would break up and she would start seeing someone else. It would freak me out and I would rush back in. Then things would get steady and I would run.

This went on for six years. All through the Sounds of Liberty and singing with Truth. All during my time with Kirk Franklin. Together. Apart. On again, then off. I'm sure my actions were very confusing to her. They were even confusing to me.

Eventually Andi got tired of the holding on and letting go. She cared about me, but I had broken her trust and heart too many times. "I'm done," she finally told me. "Don't come back again unless you've got a ring."

I moved to Nashville and tried to forget her. Andi took a job on campus and did her best to move on. I sank myself into my career and got sucked in by the Music City scene. I felt completely lost and alone, and all I could think about was my best friend—missing her support, wondering what she was doing, how she was.

The loneliness was driving me crazy. One day I couldn't take it anymore. I drove to Tiffany & Co. in the Green Hills Mall and bought a diamond ring. The blue box. I had to go all the way.

I traveled back to Virginia and took her to Jazz Street Grill, our old favorite restaurant. She didn't talk much, but the look she was giving me across the table said enough. *Why are you even here, Anthony? What do you want from me?*

The shrimp pasta came. The waitress lit candles. I was so nervous my leg was bouncing, rattling the table against the tile floor. "Okay," I said, "let's pray."

While her head was bowed, I snuck the box from Tiffany's onto the table. We said "amen," she opened her eyes, and in true Andi fashion, she didn't even acknowledge the ring. After six years of mind games, no little blue box was going to be enough. It wasn't about the box. She just stared at me, waiting to hear what I had to say.

I took a long breath before letting it all out. "You told me not to come back without a ring, and I know it's been a while and I know it's kind of weird to just show up this way, but we've been through so much and I know we don't need another dinner or a movie or some random surprise date night. We need things to change. I want things to change. So, the question I want to ask you is . . . will you marry me?"

Even in that pause I started to think about the ways I was letting her down. I didn't ask her mom's permission first, and I should have. When I'd rehearsed my proposal, it had sounded much better. I was still so scattered and unsure of myself.

She said yes anyway.

And slowly but surely, even through her poker face, she got excited. Not like jumping-on-her-chair excited. But in her own tough-girl way.

There were arrangements to make and complications to work

through. But she told her family and friends the good news and made the decision to move to Nashville.

It was all so fast. You can get caught up in the thrill of change. You can get so carried away with the new, it might make you think you've thrown those old demons off the trail. But old demons aren't so easily shaken. You cannot outrun yourself.

I bought a house in Nashville's best suburb. We made arrangements for a destination wedding in Tahoe, deposits paid. She packed a U-Haul, moved everything she owned five hundred miles, and started looking for a job. Talk about a leap of faith.

And then things went dark real quick. Issues. Fear. Anxiety. Suddenly we were fighting all the time. She would push, just needing answers and assurance I couldn't give. I still had those unrealistic expectations hanging over me, thinking I had to have things figured out and together all the time, locked in a prison of perfectionism.

But the truth is, I was the antithesis of perfection. I didn't have anything together. I was a total mess at the time.

"Don't ever threaten to take off the ring," I told her during one big blowup. I wasn't trying to be mean, but things were crazy intense and the thought of rejection was more than I could stand. "If you ever take it off, I'm not putting it back on again."

When an Evans marries, they marry for life. I didn't want to make a mistake. Andi is a fighter, but she realized I was a much bigger project than she had anticipated, much more emotionally complex. She was willing to love me through it, but I couldn't accept that. Her strength was not strong enough to hold us both. I had to be whole as an individual.

As a pastor, my dad had done plenty of premarital counseling, so he set up a meeting to try and help. It started off okay, but things escalated quickly. Andi was hurt and unintentionally pushing my buttons. She and I were, in our own ways, like rubber bands that had been stretched too far. In that moment, I got overwhelmingly frustrated and exploded—yelling at the top of my lungs and even throwing a remote across the room. I had never in my life had a reaction like that. Dad just sat there, shocked, arms folded, staring at the wall.

The fear of rejection had taken over. Maybe the Truth director's words, "worthless and never doing anything better," had sunk in deeper than I thought. Anger rose up to drown out the fear. It felt as if my skin had been peeled back and all my emotions were left raw and exposed. The relationship stuff, the music business stuff, the kid stuff I had buried so long. It was like the room was on fire and I had to get out.

Andi blocked the door, raising her voice even louder, all in an effort to stop me. To this day, I remember her emphatically saying, "Don't leave. Let me love you." How was my dad just sitting there stoically while I felt so overwhelmed? I think he was overwhelmed, too, just showing it in his own way. A switch flipped inside me. It was all too much. I stepped around her and walked out the door.

The next day Andi came to find me. There was still a lot of tension in the air. After six years of drama, she'd finally had enough. She slid the ring off and placed it in my hand. And I closed my hand into a fist.

CHAPTER 13

THE HUDDLE

"For my power is made perfect in weakness." Therefore I will
boast all the more gladly of my weaknesses, so that the power
of Christ may rest upon me. For the sake of Christ, then, I
am content with weaknesses, insults, hardships, persecutions,
and calamities. For when I am weak, then I am strong.
—2 CORINTHIANS 12:9–10 ESV

The next morning, I shuffled through the airport like a zombie.
It was still dark outside as the TSA officers shook me down.
Once through security, I found the nearest Starbucks and ordered
a grande Americano to try and bring myself back to life.

I boarded the plane and squeezed myself into a middle row
seat. The atomic wallop of caffeine only made me that much more
aware of how depressing my circumstances were. Yet I still had
to fly halfway across the country to sing about the faithfulness of
God. How could I possibly sing about God's goodness in a moment
when I felt so abandoned and lost?

I stared out the window as the sun broke through the clouds. The salesman sitting to my left smelled like sweat and whiskey. He grumbled, reached up, and snapped his shade shut. I leaned back and tried to close my eyes, but I was too wired to sleep. So I sat there, lost in thought while the kid behind me kicked my seat.

"Seat belt," the flight attendant said, motioning with her hands. I wrestled it around me and clicked it into place. "Everything okay here?" she asked.

"Yes ma'am," I told her. "I'm fine."

A car picked me up at the airport and took me to the church where I was singing. I brushed the lint off of my clothes, stepped onto the platform, and forced a smile. The stage lights blinded my eyes. Beyond them, a sea of blurry faces waited for me to usher them into the presence of the Lord. I took one deep breath, trying to get myself together. Then another.

"I really . . . don't feel like doing this," I confessed. I lowered the microphone and stood there, feeling awkward, holding back tears. I had nothing left to give. No more anecdotes, no more cool, churchy things to say, no more notes to sing. Nothing. I wasn't even sure I believed what I was singing anymore.

Off to the side, I could see my road manager, Jonathan. His expression was sheer panic. *So, this is it. Anthony's over. This is how it all ends.*

I didn't know if it was the right thing to do, but I just started sharing the truth of my life. About the breakup and the confusion and feeling like a fake. Having to board that plane and make the show go on. I probably talked too much. I do that when I get nervous. As my eyes adjusted, I could start to see beyond the lights to people's faces. Some were staring at me like, *Uh, this is a bit much. We're just here for worship. Can we get back to that, please?* But as I kept sharing, that big scary crowd became individuals, one by one. Soon enough, everyone in the room was crying.

It's like they were longing for honesty, for someone to stop pretending and just be real. Truth is, I guess we were all broken. And for one moment, God used my pain to break through.

"But I'm going to do it anyway," I told the people. "Even though I don't feel it, I'm going to sing about the goodness and mercy of God."

I didn't sing because I felt noble or holy or brave. Quite honestly, I had nothing left and nothing to lose. Somewhere in that first song, I heard the still, small voice: *When you are empty and honest, I am near. I want you to learn what it is to be accepted without having to perform.*

After the show, I redirected my flight to Dallas. I drove straight to my parents' house and sat down with my father. "Dad, there's something wrong with me," I told him. "I feel dead inside. And I don't want to sing these songs if it's not real to me. I know you've ministered to thousands, but I need you to speak something into my life today."

For the next hour, I poured out the pieces of my heart, telling Dad that I felt like God had left me, like I was an actor on stage, playing a part. I didn't believe what I was singing, but I still had to go through the motions and act like everything was okay.

Tony Evans is one of the most prolific communicators on earth, but when I go to him, he's simply Dad. When I finally quit talking, he said, with that quiet strength way about him, "Are you done?"

"Yes, sir," I told him. "For now."

"Anthony," he said, "can I talk to you about football?"

I was like, *Do what? Football? What does that have to do with heartbreak?* Dad's a sports guy. All my life he's been chaplain for either the Mavericks or the Cowboys. "Sure," I told him. "Okay."

"What if I took you to a Cowboys game and all they did was stay in the huddle?"

I trusted my dad's insight but couldn't really see where this was going. "I don't understand," I said.

"If we drove to the stadium, went to all the trouble of parking and finding seats, and for three hours all the Cowboys did was sit in a huddle—how would you feel?"

I stared at him, silent and confused. He asked again. "Come on, son. How would you feel?"

Finally, I blurted out my response. "Yo, Dad, Trix are for kids! I don't get it! Who goes to a game to watch that? I wouldn't want to be there!"

"Of course not," he said. "You didn't come to see the players huddle. The reason you feel dead in your faith right now is because you're spending your whole life within the four walls of the church in nice, Christian huddles. You discuss the coach. You talk about the plays. You have all the knowledge in the world, but you're not executing it on the field of your life. That's why this game is no longer interesting to you."

Wow, I thought, starting to see his point. *Dad really is pretty good at this stuff.*

"Anthony," he said, "it's important to step outside of ourselves and our Christian bubble. But another thing you have to understand is that emotions do not have intellect. They can be led by what you ate or how you slept or any number of irrational things that have no foundation in the truth. We cannot let emotions control us. We must control our emotions. So even though you may *feel* lost, confused, and abandoned—as strong as those feelings *feel*, you must bounce them off the truth of God's Word, or they will hijack your peace of mind and rule your life."

Then he opened his Bible and read from Philippians 1:6, "I am confident that he who began a good work in you will carry it on to completion." He lowered the Bible and looked me straight in the eye. "Now, that is the truth, whether you feel it or not," he said. "Son, God is faithful in spite of our feelings. You've got to get out of yourself, take the knowledge you have, and do something with it on the playing field of life."

I nodded, letting his words sink in. Like my father was saying, I knew it but I didn't really *know* it. I think that's one of the reasons we love sports so much. Sports provide a lot of good metaphors for living. I was spending too much time in the safe church huddle and in my own head, overthinking things, being consumed with myself, and not taking enough action.

One way or another, I knew I needed to try and change my focus and my goals. I had to find ways to get back into the game.

CHAPTER 14

A MIRACLE WHICH IS NOT TO BE FORGOTTEN

Feed the hungry, and help those in trouble. Then
your light will shine out from the darkness, and the
darkness around you will be as bright as noon.
—Isaiah 58:10 NLT

y friend Ben, who'd been kind enough to let me move in
with him and his wife, started working with an organization called Food for the Hungry based out of Tennessee. As soon
as I told him that Dad suggested I move my faith out of the church
huddle and onto the playing field of life, he got this gleam in his
eye. "Anthony, you need to come and see what we do," he said. "We
would love your support as an artist."

My mind immediately put on the brakes and sent the red flags
flying. "Not a chance, Ben," I told him. "I know where this is
going."

I still had a lot of trust issues that I needed to sit down and talk out with Dad. I had always assumed that when it came to world help organizations, my money would end up in some CEO's pocket and he'd be driving a Ferrari and living in some mansion on the coast. But because Ben had been my friend since I was twenty, I was willing to give him the benefit of the doubt. I went down to check out the organization he worked for firsthand.

He gave me a tour of the Food for the Hungry headquarters. It was nice but not *too* nice, if you know what I mean. I didn't see any Learjets or Lamborghinis. There were a lot of pictures of children on the walls, some sad but plenty smiling and happy too. My heart was kind of breaking, but I still had my guard up. If you're a highly sensitive person, it's easier to just stay jaded. That way you don't get taken advantage of or hurt.

To step outside of my box and help some little boy half a world away was a big step for me. Things were tough in the States at that time, and people were cutting back on spending, tightening their belts. It was right after the housing market crashed and gas was what felt like a million bucks a gallon. Getting engaged and un-engaged was expensive. I jokingly asked Ben if he could take a picture of me, put it on the table, and get someone to be my sponsor.

"Dude, let me ask you this," Ben laughed. "How much a month do you spend on coffee?"

Ain't that just like a friend? Like coffee's not a bare necessity! I thought about it a minute, did some figuring in my head. Hmm. For what I spent at Starbucks in a month, I could sponsor a child. Actually, I could sponsor two. You see, I went to Starbucks at least once a day, often twice. Sometimes I didn't even want coffee. It was just a bad habit I'd gotten into.

Ben said if I became a sponsor, the kid would then be able to get food, clothing, and essentials. He could have clean water and go to school. And all I had to do was sacrifice coffee for a while.

I also had the opportunity to serve as an artist representative for the program. That would mean helping to spread Food for the Hungry's message and mission from the stage during my events. Before I pledged that kind of support for the charity, I needed to experience it firsthand. I wouldn't ask my audience to do anything I wasn't willing to commit to myself.

"All right, Ben, I'll do it. Count me in," I told him, "on *one* condition."

"What's that?" he asked.

"You have to take me to visit my kid."

I figured he would give me some line about how that one photograph of a child you see actually represents a bunch of kids. I thought for sure he would say, "You can't just meet one. The charity doesn't work that way." I thought for sure I had Ben stumped.

A month later Ben had me on a plane going to Malawi, Africa. My sponsored child's birth name was "A Miracle Which Is Not to Be Forgotten," but they called him "Forget" for short. I'd already paid up the first month's pledge and stuck his picture on my fridge so I'd remember to pray. I was determined not to forget Forget. I was trying to get out of the huddle and into the game.

The flight took twenty-four hours. I'd flown overseas before, but never anything this far. Ben and I stepped out onto a land that looked straight out of *National Geographic* magazine. Then we drove four more hours in a rickety jeep with bad shocks to the middle of absolute nowhere. And out from behind one lonely, isolated tree peeks this little face from my fridge.

Somehow he knew who I was and walked over fast with his hands stretched out toward me. I swooped this kid up in my arms and probably scared him. I was as excited as he was. It felt like my heart had started beating again. Like somehow in that dead place inside, the light broke through.

Standing there sweating on the African plains, holding this smiling boy with the mountains and the dust around us, all I could think was that this is what I was created for—not to store up all of God's good blessing with no outlet, not to have mercy and grace given to me so freely without freely extending these gifts to someone else.

I mean, I brought some fun stuff to give him too. Footballs and Frisbees and Hot Wheels cars. Just little things. Sometimes that's how we show mercy and grace.

He was confused at first, turning them over, looking back and forth. I don't think he had ever seen such things. But when he figured it out, his eyes got wide. Our translator pointed to the toys and told me, "What you just now gave him is worth more than his family will earn in an entire year." Then my eyes got wide too!

His parents were there, along with some brothers and sisters. They told me about their village and day-to-day life with the translator's help. I didn't want to be the American who flew in to save the day, but I felt really convicted. "Is there anything else I can do for you?" I asked Forget's mom.

"Yes," she told me, not skipping a beat. "We would like our dream home."

A new conviction slipped in. *I should have kept my mouth shut.* "Oh-kay . . ." I finally replied. "So, uhhhh . . . what does that mean?"

My big United States HGTV mentality had me worried. Did they want me to build them a four-bed/three-bath modern farmhouse? Shiplap and antler chandeliers? I didn't know what to expect. I'd already sacrificed coffee for a couple of years. What else was I going to have to give up?

They walked me through the vast, arid hillside to their home. It was literally a mud hut the size of my bedroom closet. I ducked to enter, and we stood inside on the hard dirt floor. "Look up, Anthony," the mother said. I did as she asked. Large patches of sky peeked through the sagging straw. "Our dream is to have a roof so we don't get wet when it rains."

The stars in Africa are beautiful. You can see the whole arm of the Milky Way curled across the sky, and it feels like heaven is close enough to touch. But the rains in Africa can be torrential.

I looked in all their faces, one by one. Forget slipped his tiny hand into mine. Jaded Anthony was far away now. Suddenly I didn't care how much I had to give up to change this family's life. We fixed the roof, and I continued to hear from Forget and his family long after my visit. They continually told me how my "sacrifice" had changed their lives. I know how their example changed mine.

CHAPTER 15

RENOVATION

Now we see things imperfectly, like puzzling reflections in a
mirror, but then we will see everything with perfect clarity. All
that I know now is partial and incomplete, but then I will know
everything completely, just as God now knows me completely.

—1 Corinthians 13:12 nlt

During my engagement, I bought a house in a nice area just
south of Nashville. I was ready to settle down and decorate and
get rid of my beanbags and mismatched furniture. Be a grown-up.
Finally! I was eager to move on and focus on things like marriage
and making music and coming off the road to a place of refuge and
rest that I could call home.

I'd been so excited about starting the next phase of life with a
beautiful wife in a beautiful new home. Together we would fill it
with the furnishings that would make it uniquely our own. Maybe
even start a family soon. But instead of things falling into place,
they fell apart. This big house was empty and I was living alone.

My friend Elisha is an interior designer, and she knew what I was going through. She'd watched at close range while my almost-marriage imploded, and she saw how devastated I was in the aftermath. She dropped by one morning to check on me. I was still sitting on beanbags and living out of a suitcase.

"I'm good," I told her. "Things are okay."

Elisha knew better, though. She eyeballed those bare walls and peeked into my empty living room. "I'll get to it one of these days," I assured her, sliding an unpacked box to the side with my foot. "Just been busy. Gotta leave tomorrow for a conference in Canada and then another in Philadelphia. So maybe after that."

"Anthony, you were so excited to get this house ready," Elisha said. "I want to help. While you're gone, I will get all of this fixed up for you. All you have to do is leave me with a key and your credit card."

Leave my house keys and credit card with an interior designer? Uh, sure, that sounds like a perfectly reasonable thing to do.

I flew off to lead worship in Toronto and Philly, and when I came back my house looked like the lobby of the Ritz-Carlton. I stood frozen in the doorway. Like, *Wow, this is gorgeous! I feel like a king!*

Immediately after that another thought came: *Wait a minute, who's paying for this?*

Who'd Elisha think I was, Usher? I'm not Usher! Money is definitely an object. I ran around the house making sure everything still had the tags on it so I could take it back. And that's when I noticed the mirror.

It was huge, nearly covering an entire wall. The frame was

made from reclaimed barn wood, covered with rivets and bits of old tin. It was weathered and worn, like it'd been through a lot of storms and come out with a story to tell. I stared at it for the longest time, running my fingers over the steel and grain. Then I called Elisha.

"Where did you get this mirror?"

"There's this man way out in Franklin," she explained. "A carpenter. He makes all his own furniture. He hand-makes everything."

"You have to take me to meet this man," I replied.

The next day we hauled a load of furniture and decor back to the stores where Elisha had purchased them. On the way, we stopped to meet Mr. Paul, the man who made the mirror. He was rugged and rough—a real man's man, with scars all over his hands and a leather apron tied around his waist. We made small talk for a while, surrounded by his incredible works of art. I asked how he made the mirror.

"Come with me," Mr. Paul said. He walked us to the back window of his tiny shop. "Look out there and tell me what you see."

Not much really. Paul's backyard was actually quite ugly. There was a rundown old shed surrounded by weeds and a burn pile full of ashes and scattered pieces of trash.

"A shed and some junk?" I answered.

"Look closer," Paul said.

I scanned the yard again, squinting. "I see an old woodshed and a pile of burning trash."

"Anthony," he said, leaning in. "Look closer."

I took one more glance. "Mr. Paul, I don't know," I told him. "If there's something else there, I can't see it."

He laid his callused hand on my shoulder. "What you keep calling trash are the very things I used to make your mirror," he said. "In fact, everything in this shop was made from that mountain of salvaged junk."

I stood there staring, thinking about my own mountain of garbage, all the stuff I'd love to hide out back where no one could see. All my secret sins and screw-ups and bad attitudes. All those things I can't ever seem to get right. All the scattered, worthless junk of my life.

Suddenly my eyes were opened and the Lord spoke into my heart. *Anthony, the things in your life that you perceive as trash, I see as art. What you call junk, I call raw material to fashion into something far more beautiful. If you will give them to me, I can take those things that you would rather keep hidden and turn them into something glorious for my name.*

"Wow, that's amazing," I told Paul. Everything out the window looked different now. But that was really all I could think to say. *Wow.*

Elisha and I returned quite a few items that day. Eventually I leased that house and moved. Then I moved again. But I kept that old mirror. Wherever I go, it goes with me. When people come into my house, it's the one thing they are drawn to.

"Where did you get this incredible mirror?" they'll ask.

Then I get to tell them the story about a man I met who can take junk and make it into something beautiful.

• • •

Speaking of home improvement (*squirrel!*), I tried to flip a house once.

It was a typical "Anthony impulse move," but I figured if Chip and Joanna Gaines could do it, so could I. All by myself. That little side project ruined an entire year of my life. I worked myself crazy between the plumbing, drywall, grout, and people I hired who pretended like they knew what they were doing so they could get paid. I lost a good bit of money. I was frustrated and mad. It's a whole lot harder than it looks on television.

I love watching the projects and personalities of HGTV. There are times I'll leave it playing in the background all day while I work. Chip and Jo's *Fixer Upper*, that's my favorite. They'll find some old worthless, falling-down shack from the seventies and I'm thinking, *There's no way they can turn that into anything good. It's too far gone. No way.*

And yet somehow, they always do. No matter how rotten the floors might be or how much of the roof has been lost to a storm—even if the foundation is bad. Despite all the inevitable setbacks and difficulties that rise up out of left field, there's always something worth hanging in there for. By the end of the show, they make the big reveal, and it never fails to blow my mind.

Even though I'm not really interested in design or building or flipping houses for cash anymore, I still love to watch HGTV because it's the story of redemption, over and over again. In fact, I think that's why it's one of America's favorite channels. Because we know deep down that our floors are rotten and the roof's in pretty bad shape. A lot of us feel hopeless and wrecked, like we'll never be worth much because our foundation is cracked. Maybe when we see some ramshackle old house get fixed up, it makes us feel like there's hope for us too.

But before every renovation comes demolition, which is the messiest, ugliest part. Tearing down walls and breaking glass. Busting up sewer lines and climbing under houses where the rats and spiders live. Everybody gets dirty. Everybody sweats. It's dangerous sometimes.

HGTV never skips over the demo phase. Demolition is what makes the story good. If they just went straight from rundown to magically stylish, nobody would watch. People want to see the dirt and hard work because we know that good change never comes easy. You have to completely tear out some old fixtures. Some things can be salvaged and others can only be fixed with a sledgehammer or a crowbar.

I think sometimes, as Christians, we try to rush too quickly to the big reveal. Redemption is immediate and the purchase complete—but for most of us, that's where the fixing-up process begins. It usually takes a lot of time and sacrifice, belt sanders and wrecking balls and a whole lot of dirty, sweaty work. But we understand that every restoration story starts with demolition. Sometimes we have to tear it down to the foundation and start fresh. It costs more and takes far longer than we expect. Sometimes it feels like the renovation process will never end.

I am not quite ready for my big reveal yet. We get there piece by piece, nail by nail. Little by little, we press toward the mark. God still has to tear down a lot of my preconceived notions and ideas. Proverbs 19:21 says there are many plans in a man's heart.

We have our own ideas about how things should turn out. But when it feels like everything is a giant mess and my plans are falling apart, I have to remind myself to not get discouraged in the process of demolition. It only means renovation is under way.

CHAPTER 16

GIDEON

For it is God who works in you, both to will
and to work for his good pleasure.
—PHILIPPIANS 2:13 ESV

I'm an outdoorsman at heart. Ever since I was a kid at Pine Cove
Camp, I've loved horses and always hoped and prayed for one
of my own. Horses calm me. They're therapeutic. Only problem
is, I'm a big guy, so I knew if I was actually going to have my own
horse, God was going to have to send a really big one.

I spread the word around my community that I was looking
for a plus-sized steed. One day I got a call. The voice on the other
end was excited. "Anthony, you're not going to believe this!"

"What is it?" I asked.

My friend told me they'd located a good deal on a five-year-
old gelding that was nearly two thousand pounds. He had gotten
too big for his owner but just might be the perfect fit for me. Now
I was excited! I jumped in my truck and headed for the country.

I arrived at the barn where the horse was stabled. As I approached, I heard what sounded like a brontosaurus stomping through the hay. I rounded the corner, and there stood Gideon. His head high, ears alert. He was truly massive. For a moment I couldn't even speak.

I had dreamed and prayed for this horse since I was a kid. Now he loomed before me. Thank you, Lord! I edged in closer, holding out the back of my hand to meet my new best friend. With a quick head-butt, Gideon knocked me to the ground.

This horse has no manners! I thought, thinking back to my days at camp. *He has not yet learned the Pine Cove way!* Then, in all his one-ton glory, Gideon looked down upon me and snorted, unimpressed.

"Welllll, hop on," the ranch foreman drawled. "Try 'im out."

I picked myself up by the fence rail where he'd tossed me, keeping my distance this time. "Uhhh, can one of your hands hop on and try him out for me first?" I asked. Swanee had taught me a long time ago that if a horse doesn't have manners when you're on the ground, he definitely won't have them when you're on his back.

They rustled up a cowboy to mount Gideon. His name was Matt. Starched Wranglers, leathery skin. Chewing a wad of Red Man. He steered Gideon around the arena, getting him to do a few simple commands. Okay, yeah. Maybe. But getting a horse to walk around a few barrels isn't that hard.

"Hey, Matt," I shouted. "Get him to move. I want to see how he transitions to faster gaits." I used the word *gaits* so Matt and the foreman would know I wasn't just some city slicker wannabe buckaroo.

"Sure thing," Matt said.

Matt dug his spurs into Gideon's side. The giant laid his ears back and his tail began to swish. Uh-oh. Pinned-back ears and swishing tail is universal horse speak: big Gideon was getting mad. But Matt had a horse to sell, so he dug his heels in deeper and in true cowboy fashion cried, "YAAHHHH!"

Feeling the spurs, Gideon exploded! He bucked around that arena with Matt hanging on for dear life. Man and beast went to war, Gideon's hind legs kicking higher as he twisted one way and then the other. Matt spurred harder, gripping the reins tight. I'd come for a horse, but suddenly I had a ticket to the rodeo. Matt tried his best to gain control, but Gideon bucked harder until finally he launched the cowboy over his head, pitching him face first in the dirt.

Gideon and me

Secure in his victory, Gideon sauntered over to the fence post and began to casually munch grass. We ran out to check on Matt. Other than a little dirt and lost pride, he was all right.

I looked over at Gideon, muscles rippling. Then I shook the foreman's hand and heard myself say something strange: "I'll take him!"

I came back later that day with a trailer, loaded up my big bull-headed horse, and drove him to the space I had rented at a nearby farm. Every few seconds I would look back in my rearview mirror, excited and surprised. *Did I seriously just buy this enormous horse? How in the world am I going to ride him without getting killed?*

I pulled in past the barn and unloaded Gideon. I knew the aggressive way of training wasn't going to get me anywhere, so I took him out to the round pen. Back at Pine Cove, Swanee had once taught me a process for training horses called "joining up." My part is to stand in the center of the round pen and keep Gideon moving. Sometimes I move him slow and other times I push him as hard as I can. Then I switch directions. The object is to keep him focused and dependent so he learns to watch and listen at all times.

Eventually, when you stop the horse, he'll face you and wait for further direction. The only way he will be able to quit making circles is by staying close and connected. This is how you "join up." The closer a horse gets to his master and the more he's able to trust, the more useful he becomes. For work, for sport, for pleasure.

Gideon and I spent countless hours in that round pen. He was sweaty. I was sweaty. We were both dizzy from going around in circles. I don't know if I was training him or he was training me. I'd watched plenty of horse trainers connect, but somehow it wasn't working. My big, belligerent Gideon must be some kind of special needs horse.

Finally, I'd had all I could take. "Why can't you get this one simple concept and connect to me?" I shouted. "Then we can quit going in circles and rest!"

And I swear in that moment, I heard the Lord. *Anthony*, He said, in that still, small, giant voice.

That was enough. I knew where He was going. I was like God's big, goofy, special needs horse. I was stubborn and hard to handle and sometimes thrashed and gave a lot of attitude if you tried to control or break me. For years I had been going in circles, searching for guidance and safety and rest. And all that time, God was standing at the center, trying to get me to join up.

I had prayed a long time for the right horse. And here he was, stomping around, throwing off everyone who tried to get close, refusing to connect. That's how I knew he really was the one God sent me. Not only did I get a horse, I got a good sermon.

So, I climbed back in the round pen with Gideon and started again. God is patient with me. I need to be patient too. Gideon and I kept at it. I'd like to tell you we both got the revelation in that moment and things magically changed, but that wouldn't be true. But with a little more sweat and frustration, we finally joined up.

The amazing thing about joining up is that after trust is established, you can use the horse at its full capacity, for the reason he was created. In the same way, I started to learn that when fully connected to God, He would do the same with me.

CHAPTER 17

REDEFINING SUCCESS

Don't copy the behavior and customs of this world, but
let God transform you into a new person by changing
the way you think. Then you will learn to know God's
will for you, which is good and pleasing and perfect.
—ROMANS 12:2 NLT

Through hard work and taking back charge of the music, my career was continuing to grow. I made a good, straightforward record called *The Bridge*. My profession as a worship leader was going well. I lived in a beautiful home in Franklin, a picturesque community just outside of Nashville that's consistently ranked one of the best places in America to live. I had two cars and three horses that I kept on a three-hundred-acre farm near my house.

On paper, my life was looking pretty good. And I was still totally miserable inside.

One day I was driving through the Cool Springs area of Nashville, right in the epicenter of Christian Hollywood. Everything

I thought I wanted was all around me, and yet somehow I still felt completely lost. *God, this cannot be what success feels like,* I prayed.

I thought about that part in the Bible that asks, "What is it worth if a man gains the world but loses his soul?" I'm not talking about losing my salvation. I think what that verse really means is this: What if you attain the picture of success and lose yourself in the process?

Depression easily got the best of me again. I would go to sleep at six in the evening and not get out of bed at all the next day. The slightest thing could bring me to tears. It was frustrating to be asking God to show me His will and still feel so moody and weak.

Instead of the pain pushing me toward God, once again, I let it push me away. When I needed to pray the most, it seemed like prayer was the hardest thing in the world to do. I felt like I was a letdown, so why bother God? Which ultimately led to me spiraling further and further down.

The lows became too low. At wit's end, I finally decided to do a short stint on an antidepressant to try and stabilize my mood. It felt like I was doing something wrong, like I had to take a pill because I didn't believe enough in the power of prayer. I was conflicted but willing to try it as a last resort.

Even as I struggled so deeply, I still had to go sing about the joy and promise of living the Christian life.

Don't get me wrong, the music industry is not total smoke and mirrors, and not every Christian in Nashville is a fake. There are good people everywhere. Thank God, one of my best friends, Michael Boggs, saw my distress and took me to see a preacher at a local church where I would occasionally lead worship.

I knew I had to trust someone, so I spilled it all out, everything. It took a long time. The preacher told it to me straight. "Emotionally, physically, and spiritually you won't make it another year in this place. You are headed for a complete breakdown. Go back home and talk to your pastor."

I couldn't believe that this is where my journey had taken me. Back home was still Dallas. My pastor was still my dad. Once again, the prodigal Evans son dragged himself up the driveway and through the door. What was different this time? I was exploring options outside of the church huddle. I was trying not to let my emotions drive the train. I had changed my focus and accomplished things I thought would make me happy, but in the end, it didn't seem like enough. How many times can the prodigal come home?

Again, Dad was waiting with open arms. "Anthony, you've experienced the end result of chasing approval and the world's definition of success," he said. "Your only choice is to change your definition of success. Culture defines success by applause, awards, and bank accounts. But even the biggest star cannot write a check for peace. If you want true success, you must follow your calling, accompanied by opportunity—and use peace as the compass that leads you toward your next right step."

I knew my father was right. I needed a major change. But I just couldn't figure out where to start.

CHAPTER 18

THE APOLOGY

My heart is like wax, melting within me.
—Psalm 22:14 NLT

It was nine p.m. on a Thursday night. I was back staying at my parents' house for a while, just to try and get my feet underneath me again. Twenty-seven years old on the backside of a broken engagement, heart and spirit crushed. You meet that right person, certain they're the one God sent, and believe you've finally got your life on track. Marriage, family. A successful career. Settling in, settling down.

But for some reason, things don't work out. You question yourself. You question God. Twenty-seven is already late to start a family. I wondered if I would ever get my life together, if I wasn't just destined to live wandering and alone.

I could hear my mom and dad down the hall, discussing an upcoming ministry trip. They were getting ready for bed, talking and sharing the details of their life together. I wondered if they were disappointed in me, if I had let them down. I wondered what it would be like if I just went to my parents and finally told them the truth. At this point, what else did I have to lose?

I knocked at their bedroom door. I wanted to be respectful, grateful. My father's guidance and support was appreciated more than he could know. But in my own stumbling way, I had to get the words out.

"A lot of things . . . growing up," I began. "I know you meant well. And I know feelings aren't necessarily reality. But a lot of times, it just really hurt."

They sat on the edge of their bed. "Like what, Anthony?" my father asked.

I spilled it all out, the loneliness and depression, how a growing ministry and their determination to get me a quality education sometimes took precedence over our time together. The way I felt seeing his car drive away when he'd leave me at camp or my aunt's house.

I rambled about my desire to study animal science and how I really just wanted them to show more interest in me. I told them that while they were thanking God I was a low-maintenance kid who didn't require much attention, I was wondering why I had to act up to get it. I explained that a lot of times, I was keeping quiet just to keep the peace. But keeping quiet was killing me.

Ministers aren't perfect. Even the best parents unintentionally do things that are unsettling somewhere along the way. You grow up and figure out your mom and dad are human. They make mistakes. But at some point, you get it out in the open and believe there's grace for the mistakes we make along the way.

All that stuff I had bottled up sounded a lot different once I started getting it off my heart and out of my head. It was messy, but at least I was telling them how I felt. I talked for more than an hour. There was plenty more to say, but it felt like I'd said enough for one night.

I walked back to my room and lay in bed staring at the ceiling. The same bed I grew up in. Nearly thirty and still sleeping in my same old room.

I heard footsteps coming down the hall. I knew that sound. My father's footsteps. They would often end with the door flying open and that booming preacher voice. "Up, up!" or "Clean your room!"

Same steps. Same anticipation, even after all these years.

He knocked first. "Anthony?" my dad whispered. "You still up?"

"Yes sir," I replied.

He stepped inside the door. "I never knew you felt that way," he said. "I'm so sorry. I would never want to do anything to hurt you."

There was no rebuke, no justification. No sermon or preacher sayings. Just humble and honest regret. It was like he was giving me permission to stop pretending. To stop feeling like a failure because I couldn't fill his shoes.

Proverbs says the words we speak have the power to destroy and the power to build up, to tear down or build a bridge. That night my father's words broke up the stony ground around my heart. In that moment, I saw him for who he was—not the world-wide minister, not Dr. Tony Evans, not the "pastor to pastors." He was just a man trying to do the best he could do for his son.

"It's okay, Dad," I told him. "I know."

CHAPTER 19

PROGRESS OVER PRIDE

A plan (motive, wise counsel) in the heart of a man is like
water in a deep well, but a man of understanding draws it out.
—PROVERBS 20:5 AMP

Growing up, I hated math. I remember sitting on my couch as a ten-year-old kid and being frustrated with my math homework to the point of tears. Even though I felt like I was trying my best, I could not understand how things worked.

Life had become like math to me. Despite my best efforts, I could not figure it out. Everything felt like some unsolvable algebra problem with a blackboard full of x's and y's to the power of z. Nothing made sense. Everybody else in class understood it. But the formulas that provided other people answers never seemed to work for me.

Just like math, I came to a point where I realized I was not going to make it based on my own abilities. I'd have to be that slow kid in class who required special attention. Moving forward would require a tutor. I would have to reach out, admit I didn't have it all together, and take a chance on judgment by being transparent. I would have to choose progress over pride.

A lot of Bible Belt Christians aren't really down with the counseling scene. Which is a hard thing to put on people, really. If you're trying to get in better physical shape, there's no shame in working with a trainer. If you're not good with money, it's wise to hire a financial planner. So why not have a coach to help you get emotionally well?

The concept of counseling is more accepted in evangelical churches now—but back then? You might as well be seeing a palm reader. But at some point, progress over pride means you open your mind. If you are hurting badly enough, you will try most anything to get unstuck.

Through the connection of friends, I found a faith-based group therapy program out in the Tennessee hills. Sometimes, especially for Christians, there's a lot of pressure to act like you're doing better than you really are. Success attracts success. The stink of desperation and failure drives people away. Everybody wants to be upwardly mobile. We all try to hide our weaknesses, don't we?

Our counselor's name was Marc, and he had worked with many big-name Christian artists, so that made me feel a little safer. The other group members started going around the circle sharing their backgrounds and the issues they faced. After I listened for a while, I realized that I was not the only one who had been putting up a front.

I thought back to Swanee's lesson about how it was necessary to stir a horse's dirt to the surface in order to get him clean. I knew if I was going to really do this, I would have to stir up the dirt inside of me.

Our group of guys kept meeting. Over time, I started to peel back the layers and share more of the truth of who I was and the depths of all my struggles. At first, therapy overwhelmed me. *I can't do this!* All those old problems seem mountain-sized when you start stirring them to the surface. It was a lot easier listening than speaking, because you feel sure that people will judge. The Devil assures you that your struggles are a lot uglier than everyone else's.

We had a retreat one weekend, just our little group. Marc said we were going to get down to the serious work. We started with an exercise where you had to sit and stare another guy in the eyes. I was a little apprehensive. It was a lot harder than it sounds, to lock eyes with some other person without wanting to laugh nervously or look away, to just sit there and let them see inside you.

We did other group activities like trust falls, a random game of Red Rover, and a really difficult exercise where we had to write down and explain our most embarrassing moment. I know it sounds kind of corny, but some of that stuff really works.

At one point Marc told us we were going to try some role play, and I was like, *Do what?* "Okay, each of you is going to take a turn," he explained. "We are going to choose one of your peers to represent your major issues and then place them around you where you feel those issues are situated in your life." Marc clapped his hands like he was ready to get down to business and looked around the circle. "Anthony, how about you go first?"

"Ummm, okay," I (reluctantly) agreed.

First, I picked the biggest guy in the group to represent all my unsolvable problems, the places where I felt stuck, the depression and insecurities, the feeling that I was unwanted, that I would never fit in or belong. I put him in a black vest to signify that they were a dark presence in my life.

Next, I chose someone to play the role of Andi, my former fiancée, and placed that person right in front, between me and my issues. Andi got a red vest. Looking back, it's interesting that red is a bold color that demands attention. I didn't realize what I was doing at the time, but it's like I recognized I couldn't focus on my issues because something so bold was between me and what I needed to be working on.

Marc told the guy representing my problems to start talking to me, saying what all those dark things might say. "You're never gonna get rid of me," the man in the black vest insisted. "I will always be right here."

Then Marc told the guy playing Andi to speak. "Fix your issues!" he said. "Pay attention to me! Why can't you get it together?"

I was starting to feel the pressure. Pressure from my relationships, pressure from the music business, pressure from my problems, pressure from all those old broken places that never healed. Marc told them to keep coming toward me.

I was too white for gospel and too black for CCM. I made bad decisions about who to befriend and got stabbed in the back. I could never make things work with Andi. I did not seem to fit anywhere, and I desperately wanted to belong.

No matter how hard I tried, my life was unfixable. And all that stuff the church promised about having enough faith or praying the right prayer or memorizing the right Bible verse—all of that only made me feel that much more incapable. Like something really, *really* bad must be wrong with me.

My issues kept pressing in. Marc was pushing me. And I hate feeling pushed. "How does this make you feel, Anthony?" he asked.

He handed me a tennis racket and pointed to a stack of couch pillows. My problems were on top of me, getting louder, talking at the same time. Marc asked the question again: "How does this make you feel?"

Never in my life have I had an explosion like that moment. It was like Bruce Banner turning into the Hulk. I started slamming that pillow so hard. If anyone had gotten in the way, I would have cracked their skull. That's how much rage I had bottled up inside.

Marc didn't seem shocked or upset. It's like that was the reaction he was looking for. Like he knew that's what I needed to let go.

I finally settled down. It felt like the worst of the poison was out. In a calm voice, Marc asked, "Anthony, where is God?"

There was a group member in white, and I had placed him behind me. I do not even know why. Marc continued to explain. "You've put your issues in front of you, and that's all you can see right now. You have lost sight of God, and that's why you feel so lost."

I thought the lesson was over, but Marc nodded for my issues to start up again. They were back, closing in, and I could feel the anxiety rising. Marc told the person playing the role of God to do whatever felt right in the moment. He slowly turned me toward him. "You are loved," he said. "I will take you just like you are."

My issues began to shout louder, up in my face. In that moment, I had to choose who I would listen to. But before I could, God turned me back again. "Anthony, look at me," he said. "You. Are. Loved." Then he grabbed me and pulled me into his arms.

Suddenly, I understood. I had given my problems a megaphone and set the Lord behind me. And the whole time He was saying, *Anthony, life is not algebra, son. Just put your eyes on me.*

That crying I did while hugging God? Those were better tears. There was no hiding my true self, even if I tried to put Him a million miles away. He had already seen my worst. He already knew me and He loved me anyway. And if this fragile, messed-up, human person playing the part of God could say these things, how much more my Father in heaven above?

For that one small moment, we were not acting. God was speaking through him, through Marc, through everybody there to help me. For the first time in my life, I had shown people who I really was, letting them see my ugliest, messiest self. And the message I got back was that I was loved and accepted still.

I drove away from that retreat feeling a thousand pounds lighter, thinking, *Okay, maybe this is a place to begin.*

PART 3

HOLLYWOOD

CHAPTER 20

THE VOICE

Sing unto the LORD a new song, and his praise from the
end of the earth, ye that go down to the sea, and all
that is therein; the isles, and the inhabitants thereof.
—ISAIAH 42:10 KJV

I have a bad habit of leaving the TV on while I sleep. It was about two a.m., and a random news station was playing low in the background. I stirred a bit and heard the anchor say something about a new singing competition show that was going to be airing on NBC soon. Kind of like the next *American Idol*, they said, but looking for vocal ability over image or hype. Anyone could try out. There was no age limit, and you didn't have to be an amateur. I went back to sleep and didn't even remember the announcement until a few days later.

A quick Google search told me you could audition for the show by sending in a link to a YouTube performance. Why not? I could make a quick video right at my kitchen table. In one of my hyperactive, over-excited moments, I recorded a quick rendition of the old Bob Dylan song, "To Make You Feel My Love." I didn't even put on a clean shirt. If the show was all about singing, maybe it was better not to be too polished. I hit *send* and didn't give it another thought.

A week later I got an email asking if I would like to meet up with casting when they passed through Nashville. To tell the truth, I was shocked. I really didn't expect to hear back at all.

A few months passed, and the day for my tryout came. The staff was very supportive and kind. I stepped up and started to sing—no instruments, just me, first taking on the Bruno Mars hit "Grenade."

"That song is too high," the casting director said. "Try something else."

If I was nervous before, my needle was in the red now. I cleared my throat and tried Bob Dylan again. A few lines in, the casting director threw down her pen and held up her hand for me to stop.

Oh, no! I thought. *I've been doing this professionally for years, but that doesn't matter . . . here comes the rejection! This is what all those losers on the other TV talent shows felt like.*

"Why are you nearly thirty and I've never heard of you?" she demanded. She seemed sort of mad, but it sounded like a compliment. I wasn't sure how she expected me to reply. So, I stood there in shock, trying to think of what to say.

Her question started sinking in, and I began to realize how confined my faith and career had been up to that point. It was one of the most encouraging things I'd ever heard—but also one of the most challenging. What I thought was rejection quickly turned into a moment of redirection. The head of casting had basically said to me: *Time is passing! Why have you not taken your message outside of your narrow world?*

The callback came a month later. This new show would be called *The Voice*, and they wanted me in Los Angeles in a few weeks for the first season of what they promised would be a groundbreaking show. Only problem was, I already had a calendar full of ministry events booked. "I'm so sorry," I told them. "But I can't make it. I'm already scheduled for my own concerts and nights of worship."

I thanked them from the heart, apologized, and gave them my final no. Deep down, I was disappointed. It seemed like this door that God had opened was closing shut.

• • •

The Voice was every bit as big as the producers promised. I watched each episode that first season, wondering what would have happened, what might have been. I thought back to the director's words again: *Why haven't you taken your message out of your narrow world?* Guess I would never know.

I carried on with ministry, traveling, leading worship, and performing concerts. A few months after the finale, my phone rang. It was *The Voice*. "Anthony, we've been greenlit for a second season," the production assistant said. "Would you consider submitting an audition tape to us again?"

I couldn't believe they were calling me back. I thought turning them down would ruin any future chance. "Seriously?" I replied. "Are you for real?"

I had a lot of anxiety about doing something that far outside of the typical Christian circle. Hollywood, California, secular superstars. I'd have to sing songs that weren't gospel on network TV. I wasn't sure how the church crowd might react. Or what my father might think. So I ran the idea past him first.

"As long as you don't compromise your faith," he said, "go and have an amazing time." *For real, Dad?* After my experience in Nashville where I nearly fell headlong into a full breakdown and crisis of faith? Did he hear me say the gig was in *Hollywood*?

Still, Dad's confidence in my ability gave me the courage I needed.

CHAPTER 21

REAL TALK

So here's what I want you to do, God helping you: Take your
everyday, ordinary life—your sleeping, eating, going-to-work,
and walking-around life—and place it before God as an offering.
—ROMANS 12:1 MSG

t was a week or so into *The Voice*, and I was one of at least a
hundred others sequestered in a Burbank hotel to learn what my
fate as a contestant would be.

The path to the stage is intense. Long practices, auditions, tons
of paperwork. They had to make sure we weren't going to snap
under the pressure of live TV. I'm sworn to secrecy on a lot of what
we went through, but there were times when I wasn't sure if I was
at a talent audition or an inescapable summer camp with super nice
guards and great acoustics.

Dinnertime comes, and I'm starving. They make sure everyone
is taken care of at a great restaurant in the lobby.

I head downstairs. Everywhere I look there are contestants

from the show. Most are hanging out in the bar, so that's where I head. A big sign at the door says: "Happy Hour!" I hesitate and take a look around. There are a few people eating, so I guess they've got food. If you eat in a bar, does that make it a restaurant?

It feels weird to be going from the church pulpit back home to happy hour at a hotel bar—but that's where my fellow contestants are, so I make my way through the crowd, searching for a familiar face.

Everybody's shoulder to shoulder, no seats open. It's the most eclectic group you can imagine: a country guy in boots and a giant Stetson talking to a girl with a purple Mohawk while the fella beside them looks like he stepped right out of Woodstock. Me, I'm dressed conservatively in khakis and TOMS, standing in the corner feeling awkward.

Finally, I spot an open seat next to a girl I haven't seen before. She's got dark hair and a mysterious folkie vibe, and I think to myself, *I'm going to try to make a friend.* She gives me a sideways look at first and I almost keep walking, but then she smiles crooked and nods for me to sit.

I introduce myself, and we dive into the stuff everyone else is discussing too. *What are you singing? Whose music do you like? Oh, my gosh, I don't know which coach I'm hoping will pick me. I mean, this could affect the whole rest of my life . . .*

We go through the motions, making small talk about the show. As much as I'm hungry for real food, it's nice to have some real conversation too.

I order dinner, something low carb to try and offset that fifteen pounds they say the TV cameras add. She says her name is Carrie and she's from the East Coast, a whole different world from mine.

Dad said to get out of the nice church huddle. Okay, here I am. Only, I've got the ball tucked and I'm running, but I don't know which team is mine. I'm not even sure I know where the field is. And I'm honestly too brain-dead and hungry right now to pretend to be someone I'm not.

So I just start talking. I tell her that I lead worship back home and my whole life has been centered around church and faith and my wonderful, crazy family. I tell her how weird it is to be sitting in a bar, sharing personal stuff with somebody so different from me. I even confess that I'm actually a pretty shy and introverted guy.

Carrie starts to open up about her life, too, telling me she was adopted and that her mom had a lot of mental health issues. Church was a part of her life early on, but now it's not her thing. We keep talking, laying it all out there, and I end up having one of the deepest, most honest conversations of my life. As different as we are, it seems like we're a lot the same too. Like maybe being honest is more important than being religious? All I know is I was feeling lonely and hungry and now things are good.

After that, Carrie and I continued to hang out while locked in the hotel by the TV police. At one point she said, "Hey, play me some of your music." I cued up a track and handed her headphones. She put them on, bobbed her head, and handed them back to me four minutes and thirty-three seconds later.

"Man, that was a good song," Carrie told me. "It just says Jesus too much."

I laughed out loud. I'd never heard anyone say something that bold. I explained that there was a reason my music mentioned Jesus so much. I told her why—what Jesus means to me.

I'd love to say she saw the light and gave her heart to the Lord right then and there, but that's not Carrie's story. The encounter did not change her, but it sure changed me. I think sometimes Christians get too caught up in feeling like everybody we meet has to be radically changed. What if sometimes we're the ones that need changing?

Sharing one's faith isn't like a headfirst jump into a cold lake, anyway. It's more like an airplane on a runway. Sometimes there's a long, slow taxi before you can take off into the sky. You trust God to work in His own mysterious ways.

I ended up leaving *The Voice* a little before Carrie. She said she'd keep in touch, and I hugged her, thinking, *Well, you know how that goes.* I figured I'd never see her again.

Let me fast-forward a bit to tell a good story. Years later, I was singing at the Brooklyn Tabernacle when right through the doors came Carrie. She listened to the whole performance, grinning at me from the back of the room. Afterward, I met her in the foyer and asked her what she thought of the service.

"It's so weird to hear people brag about how their God is so much better than everyone else's," she said. "That 'Our God' song is obnoxious. You're all a bunch of jerks."

She didn't use the word *jerks*, but you get the point. I was kind of shocked until I realized Carrie would only say something that honest if she felt safe and not judged by me.

And she was in church, after all. She'd made a special effort to come, which says a lot in New York City. So I just shook my head and started laughing. Honest talk never bothered Jesus—so why should it bother me? If anybody knew how religious people could be jerks sometimes, it was Him.

Carrie didn't get why I was laughing. But I bet someday she will.

CHAPTER 22

COMMON GROUND

Anxiety in a man's heart weighs it down, but a
good (encouraging) word makes it glad.
—Proverbs 12:25 amp

Even with all my church experience, I wasn't prepared for the
dazzling lights of that now-famous blind audition stage at
The Voice. It's as nerve-racking as you might think! Being alone
on stage in complete silence, the room full of energy and millions
watching at home—but you're singing to the back of four coaches'
chairs, praying for just one to turn around. Years of preparation
for that one moment, and you've got a minute and a half to show
them your best.

I was confident leading worship; you're not trying to impress
anyone but God. But now I wasn't trying to engage people's hearts or
get them to sing along with me. I would be covering Marvin Gaye's
"What's Goin' On," and the audience wanted to be impressed, not
engaged. Christian singers are supposed to come from a place of

humility. You step back and let the Lord shine. But for performances outside of church, humility can come across as reluctant and shy, like, *Why isn't he trying to wow us?* To the audience, you are seen as less than confident—which is a huge strike against you in a talent competition. I felt stuck between worlds. Church singing was the only thing I knew.

My parents were watching from a monitor backstage. Kirk and Tammy Franklin came out to support me too. I stood in the wings, trying to shake off nerves, feeling like, *Welp, this might be the most embarrassing moment of my life.*

The set director gave me the signal to begin. I walked out on that stage hearing nothing but the sound of my footsteps and poured everything I had into Marvin's somber song. It's a restrained number, so I knew if I over sang, it might ruin my chances. I would have to bide my time.

Somewhere toward the end, I opened my eyes. Four chair backs still! I panicked and added a few extra vocal runs, thinking, *Maybe if I hit them clean. . . .*

Ten seconds left. CeeLo reaches for his button but hesitates. The audience stirs. Then I see a light. That big red iconic chair begins to turn. I catch a glimpse of ruby lips and bright blonde hair. I hold my breath, waiting for her words.

"You've got a beautiful voice and I love your tone," Christina says, "and those runs you were doing at the end—the execution was so sharp!"

My last-minute plan worked! I had passed the blind audition. In the space of a few weeks, I'd gone from leading worship at church to Team X-Tina.

• • •

They brought me back to Los Angeles that December for the next phase of the show. One night there was a knock at my hotel door. "Time to get dressed," the producer said. "Christina wants to have you guys over for Christmas dinner."

Christmas at Christina Aguilera's house? That's a pretty crazy turn of events for a church camp kid from Dallas. The runner drove us over to Beverly Hills, and Christina's house was one of the most festive, elaborately decorated places I've ever seen.

Sky-high Christmas trees and winter wonderland scenes, snowmen and angels, giant silver bells and garland everywhere. And lights! Not like the string lights you buy at Target either. Big,

Christina and me

dazzling lights lit up like stars. Opryland Hotel's got nothing on X-Tina. Her house is amazing! I was trying real hard not to break anything.

She got all excited, telling us how much she loves the holidays and decking out her home bigger each year. The night was truly special as I got to know my coach and teammates better. Some people think Christina's aggressive and kind of in your face, but she's really just a sweet woman who knows what she wants. Strong. Confident. Unapologetically herself.

At one point I was sitting on her red leather couch, just chill, watching. Christina sat down beside me. "Okay, Anthony," she said. "So, you're a worship leader, right? Explain to me what it is that you do."

My tongue froze up as I tried to find the words. A few spilled out as I started talking in awkward Christianese. She got a look on her face like, *Is this guy crazy? What is he talking about?* Trying to explain leading worship with phrases like "the Lamb that was slain" or "the weight of His mercy"—a lot of people might think you are in some kind of cult. You have to admit, if you step outside of your Christian background, it does sound strange. In that moment, I knew I had to put off the church phrases and describe it in some other way.

So even though I was sitting across from a megastar, I started talking straight, like I'd done in that bar with Carrie. I told Christina about my ex-fiancée and the heartache of ending that relationship. She opened up about some hard things she had been through. Everyone can relate to going through difficult times. Struggle makes for common ground.

But when she asked how I handled those traumatic times, I was able to explain worship, as it was personal to me. I was able to share my faith in real, relatable terms, just from one person to another, both trying to make it through.

I even confessed a little detail about making it to her team on *The Voice*. "I appreciate you picking me, but I hated my blind audition," I told her. "I just don't feel like it was really who I am."

"Anthony, I just forgot the words to the national anthem at the Super Bowl," Christina laughed. "You've just got to keep moving and move on."

CHAPTER 23

HONEST, VULNERABLE, AND TRANSPARENT

Do nothing out of selfish ambition or vain conceit. Rather, in
humility value others above yourselves, not looking to your
own interests but each of you to the interests of the others.

—Philippians 2:3–4

Things were hectic once we got into full production for the
show. They kept us busy all day, every day with interviews,
rehearsals, and wardrobe. I would record hours and hours of foot-
age just for that two- or three-minute package that would make it
onto the show. After my feature aired, I got comments from angry
Christians online.

- "I thought this dude was a Christian gospel singer? It's
  just sad. A man who was at church singing hallelujah,
  and then he's singing Adele. WOW. You can't put your

feet in two things; it's not going to be okay for God's kingdom."

- "You have a very good voice but why compromise it for songs of the world? Come back for Jesus, man!"
- "Why didn't you mention God more? Are you too 'famous' now to give Him all the glory and praise?"

It's like we're supposed to go out into the world and be salt and light—but once we get there it seems all some Christians want to do is complain that you're not doing it right. Still, as I weeded through the comments, all I could think about is how many times I'd passed judgment based on what had made it into the public eye: singers, stars, people in politics. I'd rarely taken into consideration what was left on the cutting room floor of their lives, what the unedited stories behind the scenes might have been.

Right there in that LA hotel room, I decided that I would no longer walk into people's lives—especially those who do not come from the same background as me—and judge them based solely upon what I see. It is my job to listen, to love and build bridges, knowing God is the ultimate director. Knowing He alone knows the story behind the scenes.

● ● ●

One night I was called into a beautiful room overlooking the city for a televised coaching session with Christina and my song advisor, Jewel. It was my opportunity to ask questions and express my fears. I had plenty of both as I walked in and took a seat across from the ladies. I did my best to act natural. You know, like sitting down and chatting with Christina Aguilera and Jewel was a normal, everyday thing.

"So, what are you thinking?" Jewel asked.

As artists, they had both covered pop, country, dance, Latin, rock, R&B—multiple genres. Growing up, I had listened to everything from Andre Crouch and the Winans to Amy Grant and Michael W. Smith. It might have been different styles of music, but it was all Christian. I wasn't quite sure how a gospel singer crossing over on a show like *The Voice* might do. I asked for their thoughts.

"I think you can do anything as long as it's authentic to you," Jewel began. "The audience is very educated when it comes to smelling a rat. They know when it's a media maneuver, so never sing for vanity. Make it all from the heart. Bring everything from a place of truth."

I nodded, listening, taking it all in. Soon enough, I forgot the camera was even there.

"I understand that you're a preacher's kid and a worship leader," she continued, "but that's just the tip of the iceberg. I need to know that real-life stuff underneath the surface, because that's how I'm going to connect with you. Sing about real life, and it will always come through the filter of your faith."

"You can resonate with anyone as long as you're honest, vulnerable, and transparent," Christina added. "If you own it and believe it, the audience will believe it too. I came to a place in my career where I had to choose courage over comfort. You can do more. But the only way is to step out on faith and face your fears."

"Who do you want to be?" asked Jewel. "Nobody knows that but you."

I left there that night and went back to my room, thinking long and hard about what Christina and Jewel had said. It was like God sent two prophets right there in LA to speak into my life, exactly where I was living. They had given me a challenge, and as a worship leader, it was one that was not as simple as it may seem to some. People in the pews expect you to have your act together. If I expose that I'm having trouble—maybe I'm having a bad day, a bad month, a crisis of faith, even—then how could I be trusted to lead a congregation into the presence of God? How could I show true honesty, vulnerability, and transparency and continue as a Christian artist?

I couldn't help but think about Nashville and how the industry tried to make me into something I was not, how so much seemed to revolve around marketing and formulas, how the sad joke around town was that for music called "Christian" there wasn't much value placed on depth or truth. All I wanted was to find a way to sing about God and life and stay real. To not be a second-rate copy of someone else's success.

To find out who God made Anthony Evans Jr. to be.

• • •

After a month of mentoring and practice, we went into the battle rounds. I would be singing Alicia Keys' "If I Ain't Got You," facing off against fellow Team Christina member Jesse Campbell. Two singers in the boxing ring/stage and only one comes out on top.

A worship leader singing to beat someone off the stage! Strange concept. I hated it.

I stood in the dark backstage area getting ready to take this crazy step of faith, anxiety crawling up my spine to steal my breath. I felt a panic attack coming on, my heart pounding, throat closing shut. One of the guys who worked on set saw that I was struggling and gave me a glass of water. "Hey, man, you got this," he said, patting my sleeve as I took a long drink. "Just go out there and do your thing."

That production assistant was an angel, because without that water, I would have completely folded. I know it sounds ridiculous because he was doing something so small, but in that moment, because of my need, it was *huge*! So, man in the shadows, if you're reading this book, thank you for your mercy in one of the most stress-filled moments of my life.

The stage lights dimmed and I heard the countdown. I walked out on stage and sang my heart out. For a gospel singer, this is what I was born to do—bring out the emotion, make the other singers shine. Music is a collaboration, not a competition. You humble yourself for the greater good.

We took turns, back and forth, harmonizing, taking the song higher. For two guys in competition, it sure sounded like we were working in one accord. As inspirational moments go, it was an intense one. Something special was happening. I could feel it in the room, see it in the coaches' eyes as CeeLo slowly shook his head in approval and Christina fanned away tears.

The song came to a climactic ending and we stood there, waiting for a verdict. A message scrolled across the bottom of the screen from Alicia Keys. She'd tweeted live: "Amazing performance!" CeeLo said some really kind things, then Adam Levine. Blake Shelton was so enthusiastic he let a curse word slip, and I glanced over quick to check my dad's response. My friends back home said I looked nervous. Then we waited some more.

They edited it down to about ten seconds for television, but it took Christina what felt like at least four or five minutes to pick a winner. The crowd was yelling, chanting, and doing everything short of climbing over seats to cheer on their favorite. She finally covered her face with her notebook and in a soft voice said, "Jesse."

Carson Daly shook Jesse's hand and proceeded to say, "Everyone, let's give Anthony a hand for a job well done."

Carson stuck the microphone under his arm to clap. I smiled and nodded thanks. Somehow I didn't feel rejected or let down. Doing the show was my own choice of courage over comfort, and that was something I could never regret. I went in thinking God might use me to speak into these people's lives. But instead, God used the cast and crew of *The Voice* to speak into mine.

I stepped down from the stage and walked toward Christina's chair to say goodbye. *Well, this was fun*, I thought. *I did the best I could and now it's time to go back home.*

"I'm so sorry, Anthony," Christina said, pulling me in close. "But this is not the end of the road for you. It's only the beginning."

I hugged her back and said thanks. "Not the end for you" is the sort of thing coaches say to contestants to cushion the blow when they get voted off TV talent shows. I figured she was just being nice.

But you know what? Christina was right again.

CHAPTER 24

COURAGE OVER COMFORT

Then David said to his son Solomon, "Be strong and
courageous, and do the work. Don't be afraid or
discouraged, for the LORD God, my God, is with you.
He won't leave you or forsake you until all the work
for the service of the LORD's house is finished."

—1 CHRONICLES 28:20 HCSB

After getting voted out of the battle round on *The Voice*, I
headed back to Dallas, just to be close to my family. I wasn't
sure what to do next.

Not even a week later, my phone rang. It was Tim Davis, one
of the top vocal arrangers and contractors in Los Angeles, asking
if I could come back to do some work for CeeLo Green. I was like,
Whaaat? I'd barely had time to unpack! And a project with CeeLo?
He wasn't even my coach!

Just that quick, I was rolling my suitcase back through LAX.
For the next few weeks I did guide work and background vocals for

CeeLo's upcoming Christmas album, *Magic Moment* (also featuring my former mentor, Christina Aguilera).

The work was fun and everybody was really nice. Christmas albums are usually recorded in the spring. It was a little weird singing "White Christmas" at Easter, but they were more than generous and accommodating to me. When it was over, Tim called me to the side. "Anthony, have you heard of a show called *Glee*?" he asked.

At that point in America, even if you'd never seen *Glee*, you knew what it was. "Yes, sir," I replied.

"Would you consider staying around a bit longer and doing some work for us there?" Tim said.

By season four, *Glee* was the hottest show on television. But this was not a group of college kids on scholarship or a collection of eager Christian singers trying to make it big. I found myself thrust into a world with the top session singers in the industry, people who were working simultaneously on the road and in the studio with acts like Janet Jackson, John Mayer, and Barbra Streisand.

It's a fine line between excitement and anxiety, but Hollywood moves too quickly to doubt yourself for long. Hit your mark and do your job right because there's other work waiting. There is no time for mistakes, or the opportunity will pass you by. If I wanted to get out of the church huddle and go beyond the box, well, I was way outside of it now.

Glee was a machine, song after song, every week packed with music. The show was nominated for four Primetime Emmys and a Screen Actors Guild Award in season four. We did tributes to *Grease*, Britney Spears, and Stevie Wonder that year. I got to do quite a few songs on Stevie's episode. It was a huge honor to sing for such a well-respected, professionally done show.

My main job was still going out on the weekends to lead worship and perform solo concerts at churches, but session singing was catching up fast, and I was caught in a whirlwind between Nashville, Dallas, and LA. I wanted to do more stuff in Los Angeles, but the road was pulling me away, and I ended up having to turn down more and more jobs.

One day Tim called me to the side again. "Hey, if you really want to continue to broaden and stretch your career, you need to think about moving out here," he suggested. "Because people don't just show up in Hollywood and start working this fast."

On one hand, it was exciting to be a part of a major TV show and living out my dream. But on the other hand, that anxious part of me was tempted to stay in the Bible Belt and just keep doing my church thing. I could make a living and not have to be flying around so much, running like crazy all the time. We pray and seek wisdom, but there are still hard choices to make.

A friend took me to a Bible study at City Church in Beverly Hills one night. They hold services in a hotel there off Wilshire Boulevard. A church in Beverly Hills? I wasn't too sure about that. Truth is, I was only half listening at first, but then the speaker started talking about 1 Kings 17.

In the story, there was a drought coming, and God told Elijah: "Get out of here. Head to the Kerith Ravine on the other side of the Jordan River. You can drink fresh water from the brook, and I'll send the ravens every day to bring you food" (my paraphrase).

Sure enough, Elijah camped there and for a season, all his

needs were met. But eventually the brook dried up and nothing could live there anymore. If Elijah wanted to prosper, he'd have to move on.

"Some of you have camped for far too long in a dead and dry place," the speaker told us. "What once bloomed is now withering. You are hanging on to old promises when God is telling you that it's time to move on."

While he was talking, I couldn't help but think back to Nashville. For a season, it sustained me and helped me grow. The water was fresh and God provided food. But the brook dried up. I stayed too long. I had been slowly withering for a long time there. Maybe all of this was God's way of telling me He was doing a new thing. Maybe it was time to let go and move on.

I looked around that hotel ballroom/church, and people were shaking their heads like they could sure relate to what he was saying. Nearly every person there worked in or around the entertainment business. We were all well acquainted with struggles and withering and how difficult it is to find your right way.

It would have been easier to give up, but just like Elijah, I could not shake the feeling that I was born for more than what I was doing. And if you want a "more" life, you have to step out in faith and take action even while you still feel anxious and afraid. But by this time, I had some experience doing that.

So, I packed up and put Music City in my rearview mirror. Praying, hoping for things to turn out okay. Praying that I was doing the right thing. Los Angeles is a big, intimidating city, and the cost of living is insane.

Not long after I moved, I got an email from Tim with a subject line that read, "Mariah Carey." I opened it up, curious. Would I be interested in singing backup for her on an appearance of *American Idol*?

What? Are you serious right now? Mariah is one of the reasons I got so good at harmony. Growing up, I sang at a higher register and would sing duets with her CDs and radio hits, finding parts around hers, making our voices blend. Never in a million years did I think the day would come that I'd get an email to sing with her in person though.

The emails kept coming. "Celine Dion." Another of my favorites. I got to sing with Celine for a song called "Thankful" on her *Loved Me Back to Life* record. Then I got to do "Stay with Me" with Sam Smith for one of his debut performances of that song. Pentatonix, which is an a cappella group from Dallas, hired me to do some work. Katy Perry had us on a track for one of her albums. I even got to go back and do some production work with my old friends at *The Voice*.

One door opened and that led to another, and it was like God just kept opening doors. Every bit of success helps you leave your failures farther behind. Just like Christina Aguilera told me, it took the determination to consistently choose courage over comfort, faith in the face of fear. I could have been fine just going to sing at churches and worship events. But I think sometimes we settle for comfort and security when God is trying to push us toward something bigger than we know. We long for the purpose that rarely comes from playing it safe.

I've been in Hollywood six years now. Tim Davis became another mentor to me. He kept me steadily employed and even arranged all the vocals on my first *Billboard* number one album, *Back to Life*. Tim works with the biggest singers in the world, but he decided to take the time to invest in my work as an artist and worship leader. God's provision continually overwhelms me.

Tim also helped me step into his shoes as I began to get requests for jobs as a vocal arranger and producer around town. A few years ago I even started my own production company. These days you don't have to give up any of your rights as an artist. You can keep everything in-house and take charge of your own career.

I named my company Sherman James Productions after my grandfathers, Arthur Sherman Evans and James Basil Cannings. The life I live today is the ripple effect of their faithfulness to God, dedication to pursue excellence in all things, and commitment to pursue courage instead of comfort. For me, that's whether I'm grooming a horse, singing a part for a song, or arranging vocals for a television show. It is the understanding that excellence means you press toward your highest potential. Promise lies on the side of courage. You give your absolute best and never quit.

Now I am able to keep the ripple going by helping and mentoring others. Sherman James Productions books events and tours for my family, and our vocalists have been featured in films and television and with some of the top names in music.

That's how blessings work. We can't keep it all to ourselves. You keep the river flowing and pass the blessing along to someone else.

CHAPTER 25

TRUST AND OBEY

Be quick to listen, slow to speak and slow to become
angry. . . . Do not merely listen to the word, and so deceive
yourselves. Do what it says. Anyone who listens to the
word but does not do what it says is like someone who
looks at his face in a mirror and, after looking at himself,
goes away and immediately forgets what he looks like.
But whoever looks intently into the perfect law that gives
freedom, and continues in it—not forgetting what they have
heard, but doing it—they will be blessed in what they do.
—JAMES 1:19, 22–25

Some people think leading worship must be the greatest, most
blessed job in the world. Like we just float on a cloud with
Jesus all day and get paid for it. And it is an honor, a sacred one.
I am thankful that I get to live this life and sing for God's glory.
But everybody has things about their job they don't like. Mine is
getting on planes.

Every week now, I'm on at least three or four airplanes going somewhere to sing. Flying makes me crazy. I'm already a hyperactive, high-strung person. And you're gonna trap me in a metal tube forty thousand feet in the sky?

When I was a kid, flying was a fancy affair, the skies really were friendly, and people enjoyed taking a flight. Now it's like some big Greyhound bus in the sky. It's cramped and hot and everybody's angry.

Airports make me anxious too. Airports are like limbo. You're neither where you're going nor where you've been. You are stuck in between. If you're in the Memphis airport, you're not in Memphis. You're just in a big, confusing building full of stressed-out flyers and Elvis souvenirs.

Recently I was on the airline that, well, let's just say they got a lot of really bad press for how they were going bankrupt and the way their flight attendants were treating passengers. That one. Seven out of ten flights I took with this airline, the pilots and crew would treat me like I was an uninvited guest in their living room. The mood was tense, and it spilled over onto the passengers too.

So, when they made the announcement to buckle our seat belts, put away our computers, and move our chairs to the upright position for takeoff, I didn't do it. I'm a big guy and it was uncomfortable. I needed to finish some work. I was being a jerk. I know that might sound shocking since Christians are supposed to be nice all the time, but I've got to be honest. I'm normally a polite and easygoing guy, but a pet peeve of mine is being treated poorly when I'm paying for a service. Y'all know what I'm saying!

Just before takeoff, a tall flight attendant passed down the aisle doing checks. "I need you to fasten your seat belt, put away your computer, and slide your chair upright," she said, the tone of her voice like ice.

Yeah, right.

I kept working. She made a second pass. "Seat belt, computer, and chair," she snapped, looking down her nose over her glasses. I glanced at her, then back at the seat in front of me.

In addition to wanting to hear her say *please*, I also had to finish one more really important email before we left. So I just kept working.

Look, I'm not proud of this story. I'm just telling it to you straight. Besides, I was thinking there's no way my seat belt, laptop, or chair back was connected to the engine. Did the pilot have one of those ding-ding-ding alarms going off because some guy back in 23C didn't have his seat belt on? Are you really trying to tell me if this airplane, God forbid, spirals down going six hundred miles per hour, fastening this strip of fabric across my waist is going to save my life?

The flight attendant approached a third time and leaned over me, the way a kindergarten teacher might talk to her problem child. "Sir," she began. There was a bit of sarcasm in her *sir*. "You have asked us to take you somewhere. But we can't do that unless you cooperate. I need for you to buckle your seat belt, put away your computer, and move your chair to the upright position. It may not make sense to you, but this plane cannot go into motion and we cannot take you to your requested destination until you do these simple things."

I slapped the buckle into place and shoved my seat to the full upright position. And right there in the middle of my bad attitude, it hit me. God was using this attendant to speak directly to my heart. Just like that donkey talked to Balaam. Or was I being the donkey now?

How many times had God told me to do something simple and I rebelled because I couldn't see how it related to my requested destination or made sense to my finite mind? How many times did I react with a rotten attitude? I had been asking, praying, begging for God to take me somewhere. But until I did my part (which might cause some discomfort), He couldn't get me off the ground. God's request doesn't have to make sense to me. He just needs me to be obedient while I wait.

There are a lot of scenarios in Scripture where obeying something insignificant and seemingly pointless was the key to major deliverance. What does marching around walls and shouting have to do with conquering a city? That's not logical. If Joshua was anything like me, that's what went through his mind.

Moses is being chased by Pharaoh's massive army, and God tells him to do what? Lift up his staff? *There are a thousand horses and chariots coming to slaughter us all. What's holding up a stick going to do?* But Moses wasn't the only one delivered by his obedience. His act of faithfulness saved a lot of other people too.

I've always loved that story in Luke 17 where Jesus told the lepers to go and show themselves to the priests. I visited a leper colony in the Philippines when I was twenty years old. Leprosy is an awful disease. Fingers are missing. Legs are disfigured. Leprosy can make it hard to get around.

Yet the Bible says, "And as they went, they were cleansed" (v. 14).

Jesus did not heal them first. If I were one of those lepers, I would have been like, "Uhhh, can you put my fingers back first and clear up some of these sores? Then I'll go show the priests." I would have been that one leper who missed out on his healing because I had to see before I could believe and obey.

They were healed second, but obeyed first. Most of us want it the other way around.

"Flight attendants, prepare for takeoff please," the pilot's voice broke in. I adjusted the slack in my seat belt, saved my email, and checked to make sure my folding tray was secure. The attendant nodded as she made one final check. The plane began to taxi, and soon we were in the sky.

The sweet little grandmother sitting beside me tapped my arm. "Excuse me, honey," she said, "but aren't you that gospel singer from TV?"

CHAPTER 26

PASSION OVER PERFECTION

It's who you are and the way you live that count before
God. Your worship must engage your spirit in the pursuit
of truth. That's the kind of people the Father is out
looking for: those who are simply and honestly themselves
before him in their worship. God is sheer being itself—
Spirit. Those who worship him must do it out of their
very being, their spirits, their true selves, in adoration.
—JOHN 4:23–24 MSG

Ever since that Christmas party at Christina Aguilera's house, I've looked for ways to better describe leading worship, especially to people who are not familiar with the world of evangelical churches.

I started my career as a vocal technician with groups like Truth and the Sounds of Liberty. My role there was to deliver precise pitch and always be "on" vocally. Later, in doing studio work, it was the same thing. Precision, pitch, perfection. I got to the point where I could deliver any song part accurately.

But when I began to lead worship, I saw that being a technician took away from my connection with the audience. Precision wasn't relatable. I was too much in my head. The people weren't seeking technical proficiency. They needed to see my heart, to join with theirs, for us all to enter together into the heart of God. Passion over perfection, putting yourself out there and relating to people through brokenness and hope.

I got a good lesson in this early on. Once when I was on break from traveling with Kirk Franklin, I got to go to my home church's Vacation Bible School (they have a big service for adults too). I was trying to keep a low profile because internally things were a wreck and I was in a bad place that day. Somebody caught me off guard, handed me a microphone, and said, "Hey, Anthony. Come up and lead worship for us real quick, okay?"

Every step I took toward the pulpit grew heavier. I lifted the mic and tried to sing. Nothing. I was so overwhelmed with emotion, I could not even get out one word. I lost it that day. I felt sure no one would ever ask me to lead worship again.

Kirk happened to be at the service, too, and he walked up to the platform and wrapped his arms around me right there in front of the whole church. Instead of being a huge fail, the Spirit of God began to fall. In that moment, other broken people realized they were not alone. After a long embrace, I lifted the mic to my mouth, and even though my tone was ragged and rough, I began to sing "Here I Am to Worship."

That's what good worship is. Realizing that we are not alone in our struggles, that God loves and cares for us. That we are all hurting inside, and the best we can do is come before God, worshiping in spite of how we feel, receiving His grace with nothing but gratitude and open arms.

I finally got it together enough to lead the crowd in worship, and that was the first glimpse, the first time I knew. Maybe all this turmoil inside me might have a purpose. Maybe God could take my messed-up emotions and turn them into something good.

More opportunities came along soon after. I had to re-situate my mind to lead worship, to change my perspective from a performer to a shepherd, from being led by the song to being led by the Spirit. So yes, I will sometimes share—but I am mindful that I'm not there to tell my story. This is not about me. It's not my show. It's God's show, and the response comes not because I hit some really high note while the music grows more intense, but because I am helping to build a bridge and usher people into the presence of God.

Worship should be a little uncharted, a bit of an adventure. I'd rather blaze a trail and see where that leads us than stick to the strict and safer path. God didn't lead Moses on the straightest route through the desert. It was an adventure with many detours, manna raining down and pillars of fire in the sky, seas parting to make a way. True worship should take us somewhere we've never been. You have to trust, to step out of the boat and onto the waves, to get out of the box and move on to an entirely new place.

I am not scripted. Not like, "Okay, I'm going to do this set list and tell these stories and we'll do A, then B, then C, and then take it down the road to the next event and the next." I have never been let down in worship by following God's lead and taking the unplanned and unexpected way. But that's who God made me to be: unscripted. My weakness, my stubborn streak, my curiosity—it works for the best in worship.

We rehearse. We pursue excellence. I am mindful of the boundaries of time that I have been asked to keep. But we do not bring a show. If I feel the audience needs a certain message or to hear a certain song, I will change things on the fly.

I used to think worship had to go one way. If you have the "one way" mentality and you are in a different venue every few days? It's going to be stale. You will rarely have a real connection. Every room of people is different. Different backgrounds, different denominations, different beliefs. With different needs and different struggles, at different places in their lives. You have to be sympathetic to that. So that's another place being sensitive can help.

It's not all intangible. Sometimes it's practical common sense. If I get on stage and there's a church full of gray hair out there, I might need to sing some hymns. They might respond to "How Great Thou Art" better than "Alive." And if it's a sea of skinny jeans and tattoos? I make sure the set is going to meet them exactly where they are. The key to leading worship is empathy. If you are not genuinely compassionate and truly empathetic, you cannot reach your full potential as a worship leader.

I don't sing "my songs" all the time. It's not my job to push my product or showcase myself as an artist. You have to get past the performance aspect or the concern over how you look on stage. Some nights the monitors might be jacked and the band is off tempo. The audience can tell when you're frustrated.

But if a thousand people go home spiritually hungry because I'm having a bad day? If I tune out and go through the motions because I'm mad? That's not leading worship. I have to overcome my needs to meet the needs of the people. In that moment, worship must be selfless. But it's the balance of those things that is so hard to attain.

There are times I still get choked up and struggle to continue. But you don't hide it from the people. You let it happen and you let them inside.

Here's another example. Recently I was back home at Oak Cliff Bible Fellowship. I fly down once a month to lead worship at my old church, just to be there, to be with my family and friends. It was the morning service, packed with three thousand people in the room. During "How He Loves," I looked over to Priscilla and gave her a nod. Just that one glance was enough. My sister is so gifted with words. And I was at a loss.

I put my hand up, signaling for the band to bring the music down low. Priscilla walked on stage and took the mic, reminding the people of the undying love our Father has for us and how we should never forget to be thankful.

"Right where you are and not in your heart. Out loud," she challenged, "I want you to say the things you are grateful for to the Lord."

The room started to rumble with thousands of voices rising at once. Personal things, big and small. The magnitude of what God was doing for His kids felt very strong in that moment—how vast and deep was His love for us.

I began to tell God all the things I was thankful for—my life, my health, my career, the provisions and protections He has put over my life. Thankful that I got to stand on stage with my sister, that my family works together and blesses one another and despite our shortcomings, we love and accept one another as we are.

My mother and father were sitting in the front row. Jonathan and Chrystal sat behind them with all my nieces and nephews. It felt like so much. So much to be thankful for. I couldn't stop talking.

The power of God and gratefulness brought me to my knees. It was a moment, a church full of people putting aside their problems to offer thanks.

Finally, Priscilla began to whisper the words of the song. *He loves us. Oh, how He loves us so.* She was passing the baton back to me. I stood and wiped away tears. I felt it all beginning to come together as we sang about the awesome love and mercy and glory of God.

Leading worship with my big sis

CHAPTER 27

DREAM BIG, DIG DEEP

But they that wait upon the LORD shall renew their strength;
they shall mount up with wings as eagles; they shall run,
and not be weary; and they shall walk, and not faint.
—ISAIAH 40:31 KJV

I'm thirty-nine now and still not married. People ask me about this all the time. Yeah, I'd love to be married and have a family someday. Of course I would!

"All in God's timing," they'll remind me. "Wait upon the Lord."

I've heard the phrase "wait upon the Lord" all my life. For a long time, I thought if you were waiting, you were sitting still, bored, not doing anything. That's what it means to wait. I am not a patient person. I hate waiting on anything.

I was at a restaurant just the other day and our server was really great, bouncing from table to table, taking orders, refilling drinks. I recognized something. A waiter isn't a person who leans against the wall with their arms crossed. (Unless you're at the Chili's on the corner of Wheatland and 20.) A waiter is someone who actively waits and watches for what you need. If you order sweet tea, they don't bring you a Pepsi. If you ask for ketchup, they don't show up to your table with Thousand Island or ranch.

Waiting on the Lord isn't a free pass to be passive and lazy. But that's what I was doing during certain periods in my life. Standing around, arms crossed, doing nothing. Mad at everybody. Mad at God. Resentment chewing at my insides. In my case, waiting on the Lord looked like a dude in the corner with an attitude.

What I had to realize was those things that I was asking the Lord to do—heal me, guide me, give me strength—would require some kind of activity on my part. There is a dynamic to waiting that requires obedience; otherwise you're not really waiting on the Lord. You're just waiting.

Here's another example God showed me recently. I live right in the center of Hollywood. It's not exactly the Bible Belt, but I love it because I get to meet people with zero church experience—some who don't even know what church is.

A lot of my friends are aspiring actors, and they are very disciplined people, constantly rehearsing and working to better themselves. If you get asked to lunch in Los Angeles, you will get some salad and green juice. That's what lunch is in LA. I was eating with some friends the other day, and one of the girls said (no joke), "Anthony, I've got extra lettuce, if you'd like some."

"I'm good," I told her. I'm from Texas. TEXAS. The only way Texans eat lettuce is if it's next to a slab of red meat with a bone in it. I'm glad I can eat. We don't lead worship in tank tops, thank God.

But I asked my lettuce-eating friend why it's nonstop diet, nonstop fitness, nonstop acting classes. "Can't you ever take a break?"

This is what she told me: "My agent called today looking for dancers for Britney's show in Vegas. The audition is tomorrow at eight a.m. It's a two-year paycheck. They're not going to wait while I take dance lessons and lose fifteen pounds. The reason we work so hard is we have to be ready for the role the day we get the call."

In the car on the way home, I got the message. Noah started cutting down timber long before the rain clouds appeared. David spent years just tending sheep. Even Jesus had a long apprenticeship in the carpenter shop, getting ready for his mission.

That's what active waiting is. Getting ready for God's call even if you're not sure what the role might be. You don't wait for the call to get ready. It's too late by then. And while we are waiting, we watch and pray for the lessons the Lord is speaking into our hearts.

For instance, the other day I was walking through the financial district in New York City, and I noticed construction starting on a new eighty-story skyscraper. There was an artist's rendition of the finished building on a sign near the sidewalk, and it looked impressive, so I stopped and walked closer. I could hear the racket of workers but couldn't see anything. There was no scaffolding or steelwork going up. Just a lot of noise.

God made me curious, so I found a little break in the fence and looked over the rail. There was a crew of thirty or forty men digging a giant hole down into the earth. A couple of the laborers were complaining about how long it was taking, and I overheard the foreman setting them straight with a quick lesson on architecture.

"Look, guys," he said, shouting over the grind of the excavator.

"We gotta keep digging further down, 'cause that's what the boss-man's plans indicate. Or else the building won't be able to support the weight. Unless we dig deep, this big beautiful structure's gonna crumble to the ground." (The foreman used a much less Christian-book-appropriate word than *structure*, but you get the idea.)

I stood there on the streets of Manhattan thinking about how many times in my life I've wanted instant gratification—a big career, big opportunities, and the financial stability that comes with such things. But I didn't want to have to dig deep and do the work necessary so that when opportunity came it wouldn't all come crashing down.

I still find myself thinking that way sometimes. Like with song-writing. Lately, I've been working on a new album called *Everything Else*. The idea is loosely based on a C. S. Lewis quote. The world doesn't need more Christian music. What it needs is more Christians making good music about everything else.

Singing about "everything else" is deep waters. You might have to write twenty songs just to get one that's truly great. Sometimes I get frustrated and think, *I have absolutely nothing else to say! Can't we just use one of these old songs we've written already instead?*

My good friend and cowriter, Cindy Morgan, will simply shake her head. "Keep writing, Anthony," she reminds me. That's her way of encouraging me to dig deeper, so that the song I end up with is something of substance that will stand the test of time.

So much of our modern culture is immediate payoff, no wait-ing, a thousand miles wide, and paper thin. But if I'm going to dream big, I have to dig deep. I have to build a firm foundation of character, integrity, discipline, and patience. I have to spend thousands of hours practicing my craft. I have to press in and learn to listen and wait for God's timing.

I meet performers all the time who ask me how to get into the business. "What are you doing right now to prepare yourself?" I'll ask. You'd be amazed at how many people want the big break without doing anything practical to prepare for it.

And Christians are often the worst! They think because "God is in control" and "everything happens for a reason," it means they don't have to put any great effort into it. It's enough to just pray for God to magically open doors. If I hadn't been working hard on my singing for ten years, do you really think I would have made it to the stage with Kirk Franklin or *The Voice*? Do you think I would have been able to make a record and then another and then six more?

When I looked over that railing at all those guys in hard hats, coveralls, and orange vests, it seemed like dirty, unglamorous work. They were down there in the mud, jackhammering shale and blasting through the stony ground. Nobody street level could see their effort. It was taking place underground. Nobody cared what they were doing at that point. Everybody would rather watch some spectacular new glass and steel building rise up into the sky. There's always a bigger crowd at a grand opening than at a ground breaking.

But I saw it. And He was using it to show me something about my life. We often find truth in the places we least expect. God's got truth all over. It's our job to be open and watch.

Everybody I know who is successful worked a long, hard time underground with nobody watching and nobody caring about the results. In this day and age, we want results quick and we'd rather not have to work or wait around. But as my father likes to say, "You can't have a skyscraper built on the foundation of a chicken coop."

If you want to go high, you have to dig deep.

CHAPTER 28

WAR ROOM

Confess your faults one to another, and pray one
for another, that ye may be healed. The effectual
fervent prayer of a righteous man availeth much.

—James 5:16 KJV

A few years ago, my sister Priscilla got a call from her friends the Kendrick brothers to be in their upcoming movie called *War Room*. It's a story about the power of specific, fervent prayer— the most important thing we can do while we wait on God in the various circumstances of our lives. She's better at waiting than I am, and God has brought some incredible opportunities into her life.

Let me tell you a little side story about my sister first (ADD moment). Priscilla is known for her healthy, natural curls, and people think there's some magical secret she uses to get that big, beautiful head of hair. And there is. She cut it all off.

When we were younger, Priscilla damaged her hair with chemicals because culture at the time told her she had to wear it straight.

The more she wrestled to try and make it something it wasn't supposed to be, the thinner and more broken her hair became. It kept getting worse until one day, after years of frustrating and failed efforts, she grabbed the scissors and decided to start fresh. She got rid of it. All of it.

I walked into church and nearly fell over the pew. Like, *Whaaat? Is this a joke?*

But Priscilla patiently waited, and slowly but surely, her hair began to grow in the way it was naturally intended. Soon enough she had a hundredfold blessing, pressed down, shaken together, right there on top of her head. Many of us want to hang on to the old while embracing and experiencing the new, but that's not how it works 99.9 percent of the time. In order to experience new growth, we have to be willing to let go and move beyond our past. God's got lessons everywhere. Even in our hair.

• • •

Okay, I chased that squirrel. Now back to *War Room*. Priscilla knew about the production company and directors because she had written a book to go along with one of their earlier movies, *Courageous*. But it's an entirely different thing to step in front of the cameras.

"I'm just a Bible teacher and a book writer," she told them. "Why don't you get a real actress to do this?"

The Kendrick brothers told Priscilla they wanted the message of *War Room* to be coming from a real place. They didn't want an actress playing a role. They wanted it to be straight from her heart. And when the movie was over, she could do promotion and not have to talk about the experience like it was only a part she was playing. She could discuss the life behind the movie and the real power of prayer firsthand.

Sometimes the implication of Christian entertainment is that it will always be B-level. Excellence is not always a value that's highly considered. Since it's Christian, it doesn't have to be very good. You can make poor-quality movies or music or books and if you slap enough Scripture on it, somehow that's supposed to make up for it being second-rate. But that's not how culture works. Nobody's really impressed.

Since I hadn't seen other films from the Kendrick brothers, that's what I was expecting when I visited my sister on set, but everything seemed high quality and professional. "Hey, Anthony," the director said. "Since you're here, do you want to be an extra in this jump rope scene?"

Priscilla, knowing me, stepped in. "No, he doesn't," she told him. "Anthony has ADD, and there's no way he'll sit around on these bleachers for the hours it takes to make a movie scene." (Thanks, Sis. But I would show her soon enough.)

After three months of shooting in North Carolina, *War Room* wrapped and eventually opened in theaters nationwide. I went to see it while I was out of town in Las Vegas. I'll never forget grabbing a tub of popcorn, walking into the theater, and praying, *God, please let this movie be halfway decent so I don't have to lie to spare Priscilla's feelings.* Ten minutes later, I was so caught up in the film that I forgot it was even my sister up there on the screen. It really was that good.

Priscilla's movie went from being a side project for her to an unexpected box office smash. I remember looking at *USA Today* and seeing a headline saying that *War Room* had taken the number one spot over *Straight Outta Compton* and *Mission Impossible*. Seriously? My big sister beat Tom Cruise and Ice Cube at the box office?

Along with the release of *War Room,* Priscilla wrote a book called *Fervent: A Woman's Battle Plan to Serious, Specific, and Strategic Prayer.* The book was a hit, too, spending thirty-three weeks on the *New York Times* bestseller list.

We decided to take the message of *War Room* and *Fervent* on the road with Priscilla speaking and me leading worship. This was the first tour of this magnitude that my company, Sherman James Productions, was responsible for. Response to the first six dates was so positive that it turned into a forty-city, sold-out tour.

Priscilla has always played a huge part in my life, always encouraging me to never doubt myself or compromise my calling, but there was something about her message on the power of dedicated prayer that reached me in a whole new way. A lot of times we pray like God isn't really listening and we don't expect much, like maybe it's wrong or presumptuous to do so. We pray vague prayers, not having any way to know when, how, or if God is speaking and working.

Even though I was a worship leader, I was often guilty of this too. *War Room* inspired me to make my prayer life more intentional, to start writing things down and looking for connections, for the seemingly insignificant things that God was asking me to do while waiting for Him to move. It's like something I once heard a preacher say: "You think you're waiting on the Lord, when really, the Lord's been waiting on you."

My travel schedule made it difficult to set up an actual war room to pray. I live on the road more than at home. But whatever hotel room I happened to be in, that became my war room. I bought a journal and started to write down my own strategic prayers. Concise and to the point.

For example, one of the first things I wrote down was: *Broader opportunities in Los Angeles that will keep me engaged and growing musically but stationary so I will be less road weary and more filled to lead at my events.* Just this week, the head of music for a major network called to offer me a job arranging songs for one of their top-rated shows.

It's not magic, like winning the lottery. I still have to do the work. I was in the studio last night until four a.m., and already this morning Fonzworth (who I used to watch on TV when I was a kid!) is calling to schedule more late sessions for tonight. The booking is hectic. We drive each other crazy sometimes. But it's also a specific answer to specific prayer.

In fact, what you are reading right now is a result of dedicated prayer. I wrote down, *I would love the opportunity to tell my story in a book.* I even set it along with my other requests as my lock screen so I'd see it every time I used my phone. Then, I continually prayed and watched over it day after day in my meetings with God. Eventually, Thomas Nelson Publishers got in touch with me and made an offer that led to the very book you're holding now.

On a deeper level, I've asked for explicit healing for some of my friends going through emotional struggles and seen that come to pass. I've prayed for resolution with my own internal issues and watched my efforts begin to be blessed. A goal has to be clear. Otherwise, how will you know when you've reached it?

Look, I'm not trying to paint God as Santa Claus. There are many things on my prayer list that are still a work in progress. I'm just saying He is our Father and He wants to help and guide us in every aspect of our lives.

What if we only talked to our earthly fathers in vague and infrequent ways? How could it not help to communicate in a way that's clear? After all, the Bible says in James 4, we do not have the things we want and need because we do not ask and pray.

It makes me wonder how many roles I've missed in my life due to rebellion and disobedience. I know He's the God of second chances and can restore what the locust has eaten—but I still have to wonder.

The beauty of it is this: every day is another chance to start again. It's a principle God has laid on my heart to share from every stage and in every opportunity He gives me to tell my story. Even when we are faithless, God is faithful. He cares about every detail of our lives and wants to hear our wants and needs and hopes and dreams. Even when we're impatient or stubborn or unbelieving or we miss the mark by a thousand miles, He is still there to say: "Come on. Get up. Let's try again."

CHAPTER 29

THE CHANGE

Everyone who competes in the games trains with strict
discipline. They do it for a crown that is perishable, but we
do it for a crown that is imperishable. Therefore I do not
run aimlessly; I do not fight like I am beating the air.
—1 CORINTHIANS 9:25–26 BSB

I've spent my whole life trying to keep an eye on my weight. We are thick people, the men in my family. It's just the way we're built. For most of my life I have been one burger away from the big and tall section.

Recently, I was clothes shopping and nothing fit. Jeans were becoming skinnier and skinnier. I slipped inside the dressing room and tried to wrestle into a pair, my knees and elbows bumping the walls, too-skinny denim all tight around my legs.

There was a polite knock at the dressing room door. "Do you need some assistance, sir?" the teeny salesgirl asked.

I need my junior high Hammer pants back! Or leaner legs! I need jeans makers to stitch together clothes for people who actually eat food! That's what I was thinking, but I didn't say it. Instead, I cracked the door and peeked through. "Do you think maybe I could, um, please get a larger size?" I asked.

She raised one eyebrow. Not like the one eyebrow up because something is funny, but more like a judgment thing. Actually, it was kind of both.

"That's the biggest we have," she said, pausing before cutting me the rest of the way down. "You might try the El Sereno Big and Tall."

My worst nightmare had come true. She'd said the words out loud. *Big and Tall.* I had officially crossed over, and my heart was bleeding on that dressing room floor. No offense if that's where you are in life. But I did not want to have to buy my pants at Big and Tall.

After writing it in my prayer journal, I hired a trainer and got on a diet and fitness program to try and lose a certain amount of weight by a target date. My trainer, John Peel, was as lean as they come, all muscle. He probably had a closet full of skinny jeans. I bet he could buy clothes anywhere.

John would make me do things like side step squats with big rubber bands around my ankles or walking lunges across the park and back. Ab sliders, jump rope, pull-ups. Repeat it all again five times. There were a lot of treadmill intervals involved where I had to hike uphill, then sprint for a minute, then run at a regular pace.

I did it, but I sure was mad. At times I was so low and miserable during workouts that John started calling me Eeyore. You know, that sad donkey from Winnie the Pooh? "Let's go, Eeyore," John would say, clapping his hands and smiling like he took pleasure in my torture somehow. "Lunge it to the water fountains and back one more time."

It felt like a waste, like here I was at this gym with all these people running on treadmills and climbing stairs, everybody's exhausted, and none of us are going anywhere. You run thirty minutes and step off in the exact same place where you started.

All this work for what seemed like nothing. I'd climb off the treadmill and, in my impatience, check the mirror and not look one bit thinner than I did before. When would I see these results? Couldn't they at least hook up the cardio machines to a generator and harness some of the energy for the lights? Or maybe as a reward—if you run fast enough, the TV will come on or you can charge your phone. Something? People need immediate feedback, man!

But as I was looking at all the pretty LA people around me, running and sweating and going nowhere, God spoke something into my heart. *Anthony,* He said. *Even though you don't feel like you are going anywhere, this exercise is conditioning your heart. Changes are happening internally that will eventually show themselves externally, even though it doesn't seem like you're covering any ground.*

I had never thought about it that way. Running makes my heart and lungs stronger. It forces me to sweat and build endurance. Exercise raises endorphins, which make you feel focused, happier, and more positive about life. That's important for an emotionally precarious person like me. So, while I felt like a hamster on a wheel, really, I was in training. Running was preparing and conditioning me for the battle of life.

There are a lot of times when I feel like a hamster on a spiritual wheel, like I pray and study and keep on trying but never seem to get much farther down the road. That King Solomon guy in the Bible, when he complained about how all this day-to-day life stuff seems empty and meaningless sometimes? I get that dude. Me and him, we're a lot alike.

But if I only exercise when I feel like it, I'll never see results. I have to be consistent, even if I'm moody or tired or bored or it all seems pointless. I've discovered a secret about fitness, whether it's physical, mental, or spiritual: the people who truly see change are those who follow the program whether they feel like it or not.

And sure enough, over time, I started seeing results. I showed up to my workouts even when I felt like I'd rather be sleeping in or watching a movie or eating anything other than salad with grilled salmon on the side. Some days, I don't even know how I got myself dressed for a workout and surrounded by those sweaty, pretty people. I barely remember the decision to get in my car.

But I had made a long-term decision and made it part of my routine. Sure, I could have given up at any time, but I didn't. By sticking with it even when changes weren't visible, I was slowly able to see true change.

As I go through each day and try to get my attitude and spirit right, I realize that there are times in this journey when it seems like I am doing nothing and going nowhere. I will never achieve perfection, whether it's the gym or the church or any of the details of my life. There wouldn't be much need for me to travel the country singing about God's love and grace if life required perfection.

But if I stay the course, God is conditioning my heart. He is preparing me, even in the small, insignificant things, to return to a life that matters.

CHAPTER 30

CAGED NO MORE

Give justice to the weak and the fatherless; maintain the
right of the afflicted and the destitute. Rescue the weak
and the needy; deliver them from the hand of the wicked.
—PSALM 82:3–4 ESV

I happened to be taking acting classes in Los Angeles at the same
time Priscilla was working on *War Room*. I thought acting would
be something fun and challenging, stretching different muscles, so
to speak. A friend suggested it might be good for me even if I never
did any acting, that just the process of getting in touch with my
emotions could be helpful, learning how to work with them and
channel them toward the good.

My acting coach is well known from Broadway, and one day
she got a call from a director to be part of a new faith-based film.
She thanked them and said it wasn't right for her at the time, but
then she gave me a funny look.

"Hey, do you know of a guy named Anthony Evans?" she asked
the caller. "He's sitting right across the table from me now."

"Oh, yeah," the director replied. "Actually, will you ask him if he'll play the part of Tyler in this movie? We'd love to have him on board."

I shrugged and nodded yes. My coach nodded back and raised her thumb to me. It was exactly that easy. Directly booked for a film with no experience and no audition. But you know how it is when you doubt yourself. I thought if they wanted me, the film must not be very good, that it was probably some two-hundred-dollar budget, straight-to-youth-group production. It's not supposed to be that easy to land a movie role, right?

I got on a plane and started learning my lines from the script the director sent over. Soon I was drawn in. *Caged No More* was inspired by a novel that tells the story of a grandmother searching for her two missing granddaughters who've been abducted by their father to be sold to pay off his drug debt. Their cousin Wil is retired from Special Forces, so he sets out to track them down. I played the part of Tyler, Wil's best friend, who uses his computer geek skills to help with the search.

The director of *Caged No More* wanted to educate people about the horrors of human trafficking. I knew something of that issue through Priscilla's friend Christine Caine and the organization she'd founded, A21. Fellow Christian artist Natalie Grant had started a crusade called Hope for Justice that fought human trafficking as well.

But being part of *Caged No More* brought my awareness to a whole new level. This wasn't something just happening half a world away. It was right here in the United States, now. And there were so many kids, so young.

I believe the church has the most powerful voice in the world when we are unified and not caught up with petty fights—if we could work together on common goals instead of arguing over the things we don't agree about. Regardless of what church you attend or what you believe about the Rapture or politics, we could all agree that our responsibility as believers is to fight injustice and help rescue the lost. If we could just get on the same page, we could eradicate this issue. We could eradicate a lot of issues that way. (Okay, getting off my soapbox now. . . .)

I want to be a part of things that have a lasting change. You know what I mean? If the ripple effect is deep and poignant and strong, it's something I want to do. If *Caged No More* could help save the lives of children, I wanted to give it everything I had. So, I read the script carefully until I knew not only my lines but everyone else's too.

I walked on the set and started seeing those Hollywood director's chairs with people's names stitched on the back. Kevin Sorbo? *Wow, Hercules is gonna be in this movie? That's cool.*

And then I spotted Loretta Devine's name on the back of a chair. Whoa, wait a minute. Loretta Devine from *Grey's Anatomy* and *Waiting to Exhale*? Loretta Devine that I saw win an Emmy on TV? At that point, it hit me: *this thing is no joke.* I rushed back to the hotel to study over the script even more.

First day, first scene. Wouldn't you know it? Me and Loretta Devine. It's strange to stand across from someone you've seen in movies and television most of your life. It's even stranger to be on set directly in an acting scene with them. I was trying not to be anxious and overwhelmed, to keep her from seeing how much I was struggling to remember my parts.

Such an amazing opportunity and learning experience

I had stayed up late going over my and my costar's lines so I wouldn't miss my cues. I had it all down word for word. I was as ready as I could possibly be.

The director called, "Action!" I'm running dialogue through my head, trying not to forget what I'm supposed to say next. Loretta immediately starts improvising and going off script.

I looked at her like a deer in headlights. *What in the world are you doing?!*

But I didn't want to say, "What are you doing?!" to somebody who had acting awards on her mantle at home when I just had some candles and pictures of family on mine. So, I tried to hold it together and act professional. And even though they didn't really fit the scene anymore, I nervously repeated my lines.

"Cut!" the director yelled.

Oh, crap, Anthony! You are messing this up!

I stood there smiling, sweating under my clothes. Loretta looked me over, checking me out. "How many movies have you done?" she asked.

"Zero," I confessed. The truth had to come out. "I'm a singer. This is my first one."

And Emmy-winning Loretta Devine just threw back her head and laughed. "Honey, don't worry," she said. "We'll make it through. It'll be all right."

And that's how *Caged No More* became the best acting class I could possibly take. I had private lessons with a bona fide star, someone you could never set up a one-on-one class with. Every day Loretta (who is one of the nicest people on God's green earth) took extra time to teach me the key points of acting. Her number one, most important tip was kind of a surprise: *don't act.*

Meaning, don't overthink it. Don't feel like you are putting on. Don't think ahead, obsessed with hitting your marks and checking off dialogue, and don't think back to the mistakes you think you might've made. Just be present in the moment you are in, connecting with the people around you, doing what your character would naturally do. Own your role. Stop acting. Just be normal you.

Caged No More was a great lesson in stepping outside of my comfort zone and the reward that comes from taking risks. It was a rough start, but by the end of the experience, I felt like I could actually pull off the job. But that's because I was standing next to somebody strong who was coaching me through.

As believers, we are called to look for the good in everything, to be like Jesus and find the redemptive thread. It struck me that the top tip for making movies was true for ministry efforts too. The kind of ministry I wanted was one where I didn't have to act. It wasn't about perfecting the show so I could take it across the country on tour and build my platform. It was about connecting with people and being alive to God's moment. Just being normal, natural me. Honest. Flawed. Transparent. Messed up. Vulnerable. Real.

It was next level, looking at life and ministry this way. Sometimes it's tempting to phone it in or go through the motions of putting on a show. It's scarier to be spontaneous and put yourself out there, flaws and all.

But I have a strong Coach standing next to me who says, "Don't worry. We'll make it through." And with His help, I can pull it off.

Ms. Loretta and me

CHAPTER 31

WAITING FOR MERCY

But if anyone has the world's goods and sees
his brother in need, yet closes his heart against
him, how does God's love abide in him?
—1 JOHN 3:17 ESV

My friend Ben got promoted to a new position within Food for the Hungry as their mission continued to grow. Ben told me they believe hunger goes far beyond the table, so they try to address a person's physical and spiritual needs too, regardless of race, creed, or nationality. People hunger for opportunity, to believe they have value. The ministry's goal is to help a person stand on their own and live out God's unique purpose for their lives. But you can't focus on purpose if you're hungry or cold or sick.

I wanted to continue to support Food for the Hungry's mission because I believe in those causes and because I believe in Ben. As I mentioned earlier, he married a girl I used to tour with in Truth. We've known each other for a long time now.

Ben sent me a sponsor packet for a kid in Peru named Juan Andre and asked if I would consider visiting the village where his family lived. I looked the information over quickly and told Ben I would make time to fly down. If I was going to continue as a spokesperson for the organization, I wanted to have that real-world connection again.

The flight to Lima took fifteen hours. I got on a dilapidated old bus with no air conditioning, and we started on this narrow path straight up the side of a cliff. There were no guardrails, and if you looked out the bus window it was a straight drop.

Now and then I'd spot some wreckage far down on the rocks below. I called it the High Stress Highway. The higher we climbed, the closer I felt to Jesus, as in, *Please, Father God, don't let this bus fall off the side of the mountain. Please.*

Finally, we ended up on a hillside littered with shanties. The government had told the poor they could have the land for free, and it was packed with shacks built from tar paper and scraps of tin, kids and chickens running everywhere, and brightly colored clothes hanging out on lines to dry.

I crawled off the bus, kissed the ground, and gave an offering of thanks and praise. Then I walked around the community, holding the picture from the packet, asking if anybody could take me to Juan Andre. A woman sweeping dust from her stoop recognized him. "No, sorry," she told me. "He is not here."

What? I just traveled four thousand hard miles and he's not here? Is this some kind of sham? I guess my guard was still up. "Does this kid even exist?" I asked.

"Oh, he is real," she assured me, pointing to his photo with a bony, brown finger, then off to the skyscrapers far in the distance below. "But his mother took him to the city. Juan Andre is sick. He had to go to the hospital there."

I climbed back into the deathtrap bus with holes in the floor. Back down the mountain with my stomach in my throat and back to the city of Lima, Peru.

I located the hospital, but it didn't look like any hospital I had ever seen. It was crowded, chaotic, and dirty. It felt more like a New York City subway car than a hospital. It would not be considered a hospital in the United States. I wouldn't even take one of my horses to be treated in that place.

I made my way through the crowd until I spotted a mother

I wasn't afraid. I promise. . . .

holding a lifeless child in her arms. I looked at the picture and then to the kid. It was Juan Andre.

I have twelve nieces and nephews. Juan was the same age as Chrystal's son Joel and Priscilla's youngest, Jude. Seeing him lying there sick in that noisy, bug-infested facility brought out all my uncle instincts. I stepped up and tapped his mother's sleeve. "I'm Anthony," I introduced myself. "What are you doing here?"

"Anthony!" she said through the interpreter, shocked that I was standing before her. "All Juan Andre has been talking about is how excited he is to play soccer with you! I am so sorry but he's sick and we do not know what's wrong."

"What did the doctors say?" I asked.

She shook her head. "Oh, we have not been able to see the doctor yet."

"How long have you been here?"

"Seven hours now." She rocked him in her arms, smoothing his forehead with her hand. "He is so disappointed he will not get to play."

Before the trip to Peru, I had been praying for God to move my heart. It's not that kids don't move me, but if I was going to invest that level of time, money, and energy, I needed something more. But when I asked her why she had been waiting so long, it messed me up. I didn't expect God to move that much.

"We have been waiting for someone to show mercy because I cannot afford treatment for my son."

Juan Andre's sponsor packet was in my hand. Because I was too busy to fill it out, because I was too skeptical, he was sick and begging for mercy in this filthy, rundown excuse for a health clinic that I wouldn't even bring my animal to. The repercussions of my irresponsibility were being felt halfway around the world.

Juan Andre was fading, barely able to keep his eyes open. I took him in my arms, asking our hosts if there was some better facility in town. Again, I didn't want to play the American hero, but I felt awful and the kid was sick and somebody had to do something.

We traveled across the city to another hospital. This one was cleaner. Calm, no one waiting. I thought that was a good thing, but a look of panic spread across his mother's face.

"What's wrong?" I said.

"There is no way we can afford this!" she replied, not assuming I would pay.

I stormed the desk, frantic. "How much?" I asked. "How much is it for this boy to be treated here?"

Forty dollars, they told me. The sponsor packet was thirty-five dollars a month. The biggest sacrifice in the world to Juan's mother was about the price of dinner back in the States.

The clinic saw Juan, and the doctor diagnosed him with dehydration and an inner ear infection. After the appropriate medications, he bounced back and within a few hours was his old playful self again. When my nephews have been sick and start to get better, I take them to Target for toys and some ice cream.

"Where's the nearest Target?" I asked.

"Target?" our hosts replied, shaking their heads.

Oh yeah. Like two thousand miles away.

But we found the Lima version of Target and got Juan a new red scooter and some ice cream. He was looking over that scooter, eyes wide and chocolate all over his face. Then he hugged me, cried, and said, "This is the best day of my life."

I had dates and sessions booked back in the States. It's bad for your career to cancel things. But I canceled anyway so I could stay a little longer in Peru.

We took Juan home, and I gave him the soccer ball I had brought as a gift. There was a flat slab of concrete in the center of the village where we could kick it around. As we played soccer the ragamuffin kids from the village poured out to play along, and right there, surrounded by all that joy and laughter, I made a promise to myself. This would not be the last time I saw these kids. I called Ben back

Juan Andre and me

home and told Food for the Hungry to give me all their sponsor packets for this area—every one.

I carried those packets on the *Fervent* tour with Priscilla and told the story of Juan Andre at every stop. I talked to the people about how Juan's excitement over the things we take for granted gave me a new perspective on life. How I resolved to scale back, to live with less and give more. How there are still times in my life when I struggle with dark clouds hanging over my head—but grace is strong in our weakness, and gratitude splits the dark. You could feel it when I showed those pictures and told the stories. God was at work on something good.

Just recently I made my return trip to Peru. Some of the ministry staff came along, and we all screamed and laughed as that old bus staggered up the mountainside. We arrived at the peak with exciting news. Thanks to the kindness of God's people, every child in Juan's village had been sponsored.

The kids all poured out and we played a round of soccer on the concrete slab. This time, there was ice cream for all.

CHAPTER 32

REDEFINING REST

In returning and rest you shall be saved; in
quietness and in trust shall be your strength.
—Isaiah 30:15 esv

This is a vocal emergency," Dr. Gupta told me, her tone dead serious as the morning sun glared through her office blinds. "You have done severe damage to your vocal cords. You cannot speak for the next thirty-five days."

I sat there dazed, waiting to wake up, feeling for sure that I was stuck in some terrible dream. My voice was my life. And now the doctor was saying I might possibly lose it all. The only thing I could think was, *Seriously? Now? How in the world could this happen to me?*

But just that quick, I realized. *Because you are constantly running in the red, Anthony. That's how.*

We were raised to believe in the power of hard work, and really, that's the way I live best. Busy. For me, hard work means getting on a plane every three or four days (and actually three or four planes due to layovers), multiple events, never being home, booking studio time on those precious few days when I *am* home, singing and pushing and doing all the small stuff it takes to keep your career above water.

Some people think it's all glamour and spotlight, but what they don't understand is the lines are blurry. Work rarely stops. You don't clock in at nine and out at five. You work all day and then you work all night. You work all the time.

Because if you do have an artistic career and you sleep at the wheel for one minute? Pretty soon you don't have a career anymore.

At some point your body breaks down and you start getting sick. But there's no time to get sick. There's always a concert scheduled, an event booked, always someone needing a piece of your time. And you understand that going in. It's part of the price you pay.

I'd been singing on the road and singing back home, too, doing live shows and cutting vocals for various projects around LA. Never say no. Keep pushing. That's the way.

On a recent weekend, I had four ministry events scheduled in two and a half days. Especially in worship, you want to give your all. You can't just phone it in. You're not singing about romance or cars. You are singing to the Most High God. You don't hold anything back.

So, I pushed through sick to sing and ended up bruising my vocal cords. The laryngologist said the only way to heal my voice was through rest. No quick-fix medications or exercises or procedures. Only rest. And in my case, more than a solid month of it.

Injury is the rest you are forced into when you fail to observe the value of rest. And it's always ill-timed and inconvenient.

No singing. No talking. Do you know how much I talk on a daily basis? Not only could I not do the things that earned my living, I couldn't do much of anything. I had to cancel performances, cancel plans. Cancel a show in Hawaii! I sat in my apartment, lonely and bored, waiting for the verdict on my voice.

After further tests and scopes, Dr. Gupta informed me that I was prone to injury due to capillaries in my vocal cords that easily rupture. If I kept pushing, it could permanently damage my voice. If I wanted to continue singing professionally, she suggested laser surgery to repair the capillaries along with major changes to my daily schedule.

I was like, *Wait, did you just say surgery? You want to do an operation on my throat?*

In fact, this news from Dr. Gupta came right before I received this book deal. As I work on this book titled *Unexpected Places*, I find myself in an unexpected place, totally shut down and stuck on the sidelines as my friends in music speed by, continuing to tour and do what they were called to do. Like I mentioned earlier, I am still a big attention-deficit kid. I would never be able to sit still long enough, to go deep enough to write the stories of my life unless . . . I was forced to sit in silence. Unless I couldn't do anything but sit at my laptop and write. Truly, the Lord works in mysterious ways.

Back when I was growing up in Dallas, Highway 75 North was only four lanes, and it was always slow and packed with traffic. One day the city announced they were expanding 75 from four lanes to eight. But in order to expand, first they had to shut it down.

It was more than annoying for a while, but the end result was a highway that could handle the city's growth. That's my hope: that God had to shut me down to expand my capacity and prepare me for a new season of growth, whether it's in my career or my spirit or both. That's what I pray as I sit alone in my living room while my mind fights anxious thoughts.

In the Bible, wisdom and revelation often come from places of silence and rest. God rested from His work. Jesus often withdrew to lonely places to be still. Why do we not value rest? Especially in ministry? Why do we always think more is better? The power isn't always in pushing through. Sometimes it's in the rest.

"When you recover from this injury, you are going to have to readjust the way you do work and life," Dr. Gupta warned. "You will have to redefine what normal is for you."

One cool thing about God is He shows us so much about life through circumstances. Even bad ones. Especially the bad ones. That's what the Word means by "everything works together for the good." Good and bad—both teach us.

The lesson wasn't just about how to take care of my voice. When the doctor talked about my bruised vocal cords, I thought about how there were parts of my spirit that had been damaged too. Life leaves bruises. There are places where you become prone to injury from multiple breaks. Spots that are callused over to protect from further pain.

If you create a callus on your vocal cord, it changes the sound of your voice. It could possibly ruin your voice. There were places in my heart that had been changed from trying to push through. From failing to honor rest, from trying to follow the expected path instead of finding God's right way for me.

Ministry and Christian living are not solely about achievement. It's not all about getting to the mountaintop with our hands in the air or how many people we can corral into church. Sometimes ministry can be more about creating places of push than a place of rest. Maybe that's why so many get hurt.

I thought about that time in the Bible where Jesus visited Martha and Mary. One of my Bibles says Martha was "the jittery type." I can relate! Mary was just hanging out and listening to Jesus, and Martha complained because there was so much work to do. Jesus told her to quit worrying about the details so much. Only one thing truly matters. Get close to God.

With twelve days left of forced silence, things were getting better, but I was still restless. I drove up the Pacific Coast Highway to my favorite little place where I can sit, stare at the ocean, and talk to God. Except I couldn't talk. So, I had to listen. And as the sun dipped over the horizon and the waves crashed against the shore, my mind finally began to be still.

CHAPTER 33

PLAN B: UNEXPECTED

Brothers and sisters, I do not consider myself yet to
have taken hold of it. But one thing I do: Forgetting
what is behind and straining toward what is ahead.

—Philippians 3:13

It was dark by the time I got back to my apartment. I stayed out
late on Carbon Beach, listening to God, thinking back to all the
places my journey has taken me so far.

I didn't want to go from private school to a public one. But
that helped me find my passion and come out of my shell. I didn't
want to go to a Christian college. But that's where I really started
to sing. I didn't like touring at first, but I learned some valuable
lessons and it helped me get further down the road. Nashville hurt,
but the experience was crucial to my career.

Every step led me to where I am today—out here in Hollywood,
trying to hear Jesus over the noise, trying to find my place, trying
to be still and know God.

There's always a fork in the road, a left turn instead of a right where life makes a major change. Mine was that broken engagement. Out there on the ocean, I couldn't help but think about Andi and what might have been if I just could have found a way, if I would not have closed my hand into a fist around that ring.

God had knocked at my heart three times. *Talk to her. Tell her the truth about how you feel fearful. Talk to your parents.* But I would not do it. I held it all in. I could not be that courageous. Faith brings promise. Acting on fear has its price.

When you lose your grip in one area of your life, it makes you grab tighter to something else. If I could not have a life of marriage and children, then I would give my career 100 percent. I would do everything I possibly could to reach that dream. That's what made the difference between moving to Los Angeles or moving home.

Is it rewarding to work at the top of the industry, with top names, on music heard around the world? Absolutely. I am thankful every day for the opportunity. It's still hard to believe I made it here.

But sometimes, late at night, I will step out on my balcony and stare at the city lights and the cars down Sunset. And I'm like, *Really, God?* It feels like my heart was made for family. Not TV networks and the Sunset Strip. Kids are stressful, but that's the best kind of stress. The end result of Hollywood stress is your name running fast on the end credits while everybody puts their dishes in the sink. That's your legacy. You can't name that project "Anthony Evans III" or watch as he takes his first steps.

Fortunately, LA moves fast. It keeps you too busy to think or linger too long in the bittersweet. Most of the time, at least.

Andi moved back to Virginia. She got her old job back, settled down, and had a family. I continue to pray for her every day knowing she is happy, loved, and doing well.

I'm thirty-nine and still single. I still haven't opened that fist.

Sometimes we miss plan A. Sometimes we miss plans B, C, and D. I did not get the super-hit Christian life I heard about in all those songs and books. But that's okay. For the most part, that's not real life anyway. God is in control. God gives us choices. God is still able to bring a miracle from my mess.

I don't want to give the impression that I don't love the music, because I truly do. But I want people to understand that there is a broken yet hope-filled man on stage. Someone with the same doubts and fears and frustrations. I have not yet arrived. But I'm working on it every day. There is always a choice to get back to life. You get up. Keep going. Mercy is new each morning. Every day is a chance to start over again.

Christ means God is with us. Even in the unexpected places of life.

CHAPTER 34

BACK TO LIFE

I am convinced and confident of this very thing,
that He who has begun a good work in you will
[continue to] perfect *and* complete it until the
day of Christ Jesus [the time of His return].
—Philippians 1:6 amp

My flight from LAX to Dallas was delayed, but I made it at the last minute. I'm sitting backstage at Oak Cliff Bible Fellowship, trying to catch my breath. For months now I've been racing. Racing to the studio, racing to the airport, racing across the planet to sing and help sick kids and make movies and lead worship conferences and write a book and do events with my sister. I've had two rounds of forced vocal rest because I pushed too hard. Fonzworth Bentley and the network are still blowing up my phone.

I'm still scattered and struggling to stay focused, every few minutes like—squirrel! My life has been full-on squirrel season these last few months. Still trying to be still, Jesus. Help me! I hope mercy means we get credit for still trying.

Oak Cliff's pews are packed with thousands for the Pursuit Singles Summit. Dad's church, my church. I think about all the years past, how far I've come, how far I still have left to go. I remember those six heavy words from that Promise Keepers meeting back when I was twelve.

I can never, ever be him.

The announcer steps onto the platform. I feel that old anxiety rising as I hear my name echo across the room. She is not introducing my father as the next speaker. She is introducing me.

I step out onto the stage and start to stutter, trying to get my words to come out right. Trying not to apologize for who I am and who I am not.

All eyes are on me. This is my home church, the place where I grew up. I can feel the expectation, see it in their faces. I can tell they're thinking, *Oh, Lord. Anthony is the one Evans kid who's liable to say anything that pops into his head.*

I'm wearing skinny jeans, a sweatshirt, and sneakers. The audience is nearly 99 percent women, thank God. I relax a little when they laugh at my first joke. Laughter is grace. It changes everything.

So, I try another funny bit, and when they crack up again, it feels like the ice is breaking. From there, I start to tell them the story of my life so far.

"I'm a preacher's kid, so I know how to walk in a room and shake hands and kiss babies and make everyone feel like things are great," I begin. "But I had to learn how God moved in my life without falling back on the same old Christian clichés. Somewhere along the way, I bought into the notion that we have to get everything in our lives together before we can let people see us, especially in church or on stage. Which means we learn to hide our faults and pretend. Which means that nobody ever gets to know who we truly are."

The people sit in silence, listening. No one is laughing now. A wave of anxiety sweeps over me. I would so much rather be singing. But I take a deep breath and press on.

"Being silent about my struggles was killing me inside," I confess. "But I came to a place where I had to try and grasp that if God accepts me just as I am, God's people can too."

My throat is still raspy, so I take a long drink of water before talking again. "I am still a work in progress," I tell them. "I still mess up all the time. I'm still trying to figure out my career and ministry. Still not married. I still don't have kids."

The piano plays softly behind me. Heads are nodding around the room. The old twin sisters in the second pew lift their hands and give me a much appreciated "amen."

"If I talk about God's mercy, it's not because I'm a worship leader and that's my job," I continue. "It's because I've experienced His love firsthand through a difficult time. It's because He let me run to the end of myself, to the end of my pride and abilities. To the end of that false idol of having it together and pretending to be strong. Our God is a healer, I have no doubt. But sometimes He leaves the thorn so we can relate to other people's pain. Sometimes He leaves it because there's a lesson in the struggle somehow."

As I pause and look out over the faces one by one, I suddenly realize something. We all get wounded. Whether you were raised in the projects or a gated community, by a single mom or supportive parents who worked hard to give you everything they could—we are all struggling down here, all with our own set of strengths and weaknesses. And sometimes our worst fault can become the very thing He uses for His glory.

"God is a God of second chances," I tell the people, my voice cracking with emotion. "Third chances. And chances beyond that. Because even when we are faithless, He is faithful. God is still able to bring a miracle from our mess."

As my eyes adjust to the light, I can see up into the balcony. A familiar figure stands at the rail watching, tall and still so strong. Oak Cliff's godfather. The man whose name I share.

Twenty-seven years later, it's still sinking in. I never was supposed to be him. I was supposed to be me. Just honest, vulnerable, sometimes-silly, oversensitive, attention-deficit, messed-up Anthony Evans Jr. God's creation. Loved and forgiven. That would be enough. For this life and the next.

I nod up to where he stands. *Hey, Dad.*

My father smiles and salutes back. The people look from me to him and back again. And then they begin to applaud. I continue speaking and can tell that, in his own quiet way, he is proud of the individual I have become.

Me and my hero—Dad

ACKNOWLEDGMENTS

To my siblings: Jonathan, Chrystal, and Priscilla for listening and loving me unconditionally.

My best friends for pushing me to do more.

Tim Alderson for setting in motion a belief that I can do more.

Michelle McNulty for a few words that broadened my perspective and changed the course of my life.

Tracy Alderson and Summer Pennino for helping me with the details of this ministry and business.

Debbie Wickwire and W Publishing for not giving up on me and helping me develop this project.

Jamie Blaine, you have helped me get these thoughts organized. I am so grateful.

ABOUT THE AUTHOR

A nthony Evans has voiced the gospel for more than a decade with such a melodic, thought-provoking style that he has emerged as one of Christian Music's premiere male vocalists, songwriters, and worship leaders. His time in Los Angeles with NBC's hit show *The Voice* led him to think more progressively about his music—without compromising his faith and message.

With eight solo projects, multiple music videos, and inspirational literary collaborations with beloved pastor and international speaker Dr. Tony Evans and sister Priscilla Shirer, Anthony has vibrated the doors of the church and ventured beyond.